PENGUIN TWENTIETH-CENTURY CLASSICS

EARLY POEMS

Edna St. Vincent Millay was born in 1892 in Rockland, Maine, and grew up in the seaside town of Camden. She published her first poems as a teenager and, at twenty, her long poem "Renascence" appeared in the anthology *The Lyric Year*. At Vassar, she developed her talents and reputation as a dramatist and actor. After graduating in 1917, Millay moved to Greenwich Village in New York City where she gave poetry readings and became known for her freedom of thought and feminist views. She acted and wrote for the Provincetown Players theater group and in 1919 directed a production of her play *Aria da Capo*. Her poetry was published in several magazines, including *Vanity Fair, Poetry*, and *Forum*. Her first book, *Renascence and Other Poems* (1917), was followed in 1920 by *A Few Figs from Thistles* (an expanded edition appeared in 1922) and in 1921 by *Second April*.

In 1923, upon her return from two years of writing and traveling in Europe, Millay received the second annual Pulitzer Prize for Poetry and published a new collection, *The Harp-Weaver and Other Poems*. That same year she married Eugen Boissevain, and in 1925 they moved to a farm in upstate New York. Millay published five more collections of poetry: *The Buck in the Snow* (1928), *Fatal Interview* (1931), *Wine from These Grapes* (1934), *Huntsman, What Quarry?* (1939), *Make Bright the Arrows* (1940); a prose collection under her pen name, Nancy Boyd, titled *Distressing Dialogues* (1924; its foreword carried Millay's byline); a translation, with George Dillon, of Baudelaire's *Flowers of Evil* (1936); the verse dramas *Conversation at Midnight* (1937) and *The Murder of Lidice* (1942); and several plays. Her final book was the posthumously published *Mine the Harvest* (1954), edited by her younger sister Norma. Edna St. Vincent Millay died in 1950.

Holly Peppe, who holds a master of arts in teaching from Brown University and a Ph.D. in English from the University of New Hampshire, is a former professor and director of the English department at the American College of Rome and a National Endowment for the Humanities scholar. Dr. Peppe—whose doctoral dissertation focuses on Millay's critical reception and sonnet sequences, and who often lectures on Millay—has served as president of the Edna St. Vincent Millay Society since 1987. The Society is responsible for the preservation of Steepletop, the poet's home (designated a National Public Landmark) in Austerlitz, New York, and the placement of the poet's archives and family papers. Dr. Peppe is also involved with the Millay Colony for the Arts, an artists' retreat at Steepletop founded in 1973 by Norma Millay. Dr. Peppe's own poetry, translations, articles, and essays have appeared in numerous books and periodicals. She lives in New York City.

EARLY POEMS

EDNA ST. VINCENT MILLAY

EDITED WITH AN
INTRODUCTION AND NOTES
BY HOLLY PEPPE

PENGUIN BOOKS

PENGUIN BOOKS
Published by the Penguin Group
Penguin Putnam Inc., 375 Hudson Street,
New York, New York 10014, U.S.A.
Penguin Books Ltd, 27 Wrights Lane,
London W8 5TZ, England
Penguin Books Australia Ltd, Ringwood,
Victoria, Australia
Penguin Books Canada Ltd, 10 Alcorn Avenue,
Toronto, Ontario, Canada M4V 3B2
Penguin Books (N.Z.) Ltd, 182–190 Wairau Road,
Auckland 10, New Zealand
Penguin India, 210 Chiranjiv Tower, 43 Nehru Place,
New Delhi 11009, India

Penguin Books Ltd, Registered Offices:
Harmondsworth, Middlesex, England

This volume first published in Penguin Books 1998

1 3 5 7 9 10 8 6 4 2

LIBRARY OF CONGRESS CATALOGING IN PUBLICATION DATA
Millay, Edna St. VIncent, 1892–1950.
[Poems. Selections]
Early poems/Edna St. Vincent Millay; edited with an introduction
and notes by Holly Peppe.
p. cm.—(Penguin twentieth-century classics)
Includes index.
ISBN 0 14 11.8054 4
I. Peppe, Holly. II. Title. III. Series.
PS3525.I495A6 1998
811'.52—dc21 98-23165

Printed in the United States of America
Set in Bembo
Designed by Virginia Norey

ACKNOWLEDGMENTS

I would like to thank Elizabeth Barnett, Millay's literary administrator, for her friendship and generous assistance in all things Millay, including her brilliant insights into the poet's life and work. I am also indebted to Caroline White, classics editor at Penguin, for her thoughtful guidance, good judgment, and understanding.

I am grateful to my colleagues on the Millay Society Board of Directors for their efforts to restore the poet's home at Steepletop and ensure that the Millay family papers are protected and made accessible to scholars in years to come.

Grateful acknowledgment is also due to the poet's sister Norma Millay (1894–1986) for her inspiring spirit, friendship, and support during the early years of my research.

Finally, I would like to thank my mother, who shared with me—among her many gifts—her warmth, wisdom, and love for poetry; and my departed father, for his faith that, regardless of the odds, the good will always triumph in the end.

CONTENTS

A Few Figs from Thistles

Second April

INTRODUCTION

"To hold secure the province of Pure Art," and to create "the deeply loved, the laboured polished line"[1]—such were the aspirations of Edna St. Vincent Millay, one of the best-known poets in America during the first half of the twentieth century. Millay wrote primarily in traditional, rhyming poetic forms such as the lyric and the sonnet, though her subject matter varied widely—from meditations on nature, love, life, loss, death, and the reincarnation of the human soul to commentaries on political injustice and discrimination against women.

Millay's poetic voice, with its range of personae, defies categorization. Always, however, Millay reveals insight into the human predicament by weaving intellect, emotion, and irony into original, at times surprising, combinations. In many of her early poems Millay rejected the societal roles considered acceptable for women in America during the years following World War I. As a result she quickly earned the dual reputation of a sexually liberated young woman following her own moral code and a spokesperson staking her generation's claim to personal freedom.

That reputation was shaped by memorable lyrics such as the near legendary quatrain published in 1918:

My candle burns at both ends;
It will not last the night;
But ah, my foes, and oh, my friends—
It gives a lovely light!

and the melodic "We were very tired, we were very merry— / We had gone back and forth all night on the ferry," as well as finely crafted sonnets in which a woman speaker declares her emotional independence from men, challenging: "I shall forget you presently, my dear" and "Oh, think not I am faithful to a vow!"

Millay's writing career began in her seaside childhood days in Camden, Maine, when several of her poems were published in a popular magazine designed for young readers, *St. Nicholas.* For the poem "Friends," she was given their highest accolade, a cash award of $5.00.[2] In high school she continued to write poetry, as well as essays and plays, and became editor-in-chief of her school's literary magazine, *The Megunticook.* Three years after graduation, in 1912, Millay submitted a poem entitled "Renaissance" to a national poetry contest offering publication in an anthology, *The Lyric Year,* for the one hundred best entries and cash prizes for the top three poems. Though Millay's poem (renamed "Renascence" at the suggestion of one of the judges) ranked fourth and received no award, its publication brought the young poet immediate acclaim from readers and critics who applauded her as an exciting though somewhat mysterious new talent on the literary scene.

Most incredulous about the identity of the "Renascence" poet were two other poets whose work appeared in *The Lyric Year,* Arthur Davison Ficke and Witter Bynner.[3] In a letter to the editor of the collection, Ferdinand Earle, Ficke wrote:

> ["Renascence"] really lights up the whole book. It seems to both of us a real vision, such as Coleridge might have seen. Are you at liberty to name the author? The little item about her in the back of the book is a marvel of humor. No sweet young thing of twenty ever ended a poem precisely where this one ends; it takes a brawny male of forty-five to do that. . . .

The amused editor forwarded the letter to Millay, who responded:

> To Mr. Ficke and Mr. Bynner:
> Mr. Earle has acquainted me with your wild surmises. Gentlemen: I must convince you of your error; my reputation is at stake. I simply will not be a "brawny male." Not that I have an aversion to brawny males; *au contraire, au contraire*. But I cling to my femininity! Is it that you consider brain and brawn so inseparable? . . . But, gentlemen: when a woman insists that she is twenty, you must not, must not call her forty-five. That is more than wicked, that is indiscreet. . . . Seriously: I thank you also for the compliment you have unwittingly given me. For tho I do not yet aspire to be forty-five and brawny, if my verse so represents me, I am more gratified than I can say.[4]

In 1912, Millay's talent and potential were also acknowledged by Caroline Dow, head of the YWCA National Training School in New York, who, after hearing Millay sing original songs and recite her poems (including "Renascence"),[5] offered to sponsor her and help raise funds for a college education at Smith or Vassar. Millay accepted the offer and decided on Vassar. In a letter to her mother in January 1913 she explained her choice:

> I got a Vassar catalogue from someone today. . . . I've had lots of fun looking up names, in that and in the Smith catalogue. . . . In Vassar now there are four girls from Persia, two from Syria, two from Japan, one from Berlin, Germany. . . . There isn't one "furriner" in Smith. Lots of Maine girls go to Smith; very few to Vassar. I'd rather go to Vassar. . . . "I don't know where I'm going but I'm on my way."[6]

In February 1913 Millay left Camden for New York to attend courses at Barnard in anticipation of Vassar's entrance exams. While in the city, Millay enjoyed the attentions of more established writers and poets such as Louis Untermeyer and Sara Teasdale (who were curious to meet the author of the celebrated "Renascence"), and was delighted to meet Witter Bynner in person. She also began corresponding with Vassar's professor of Latin and Greek, Elizabeth Hazelton Haight, who would become her mentor at Vassar and a lifelong friend.

When Millay entered Vassar College in the fall of 1913, she was twenty-one and accustomed to following her own rules. During her freshman year, she wrote to Ficke: "I hate this pink-and-gray college. If there had been a college in *Alice in Wonderland* it would be this college. . . . They trust us with everything but men,— . . . A man is forbidden as if he were an apple."[7] Though she continued to rebel against college regulations such as curfews and required class attendance throughout the next four years, her attitude toward the school softened as she made friends and began studying subjects that interested her: the classics, poetry, drama, history, languages, art, psychology, and music. She also acted in plays, pageants, and other dramatic productions[8] and continued to write prodigiously, composing many of the songs, poems, and plays presented at college ceremonies. One of Millay's allies at Vassar was the college president, Henry Noble MacCracken, who recognized her talent and was amused by her quick wit. He recalls a typical exchange:

> In those days students could absent themselves whenever they pleased and just send in a sick excuse. I stopped [Millay] in the hall one of those times and said, "Vincent, you sent in a sick excuse at nine o'clock this morning and at ten o'clock I happened to look out the window of my office and you were trying to kick out the light in the chandelier on top of the Taylor Hall arch, which seemed a rather lively exercise for someone so taken with illness." She looked very solemnly at me and said to me, "Prexy, at the moment of your class, I was in pain with a poem." What could you do with a girl like that?[9]

Millay's popularity with the faculty at Vassar was tested when, in the weeks before graduation, they penalized her for staying off campus overnight without permission (when she had not yet fulfilled the penalty for a previous offense). Her punishment: she was suspended indefinitely and would not receive her degree. Millay was initially shaken by the idea of not graduating with her class, but she managed to quip, "I always said, . . . that I had come in [to Vassar] over the fence & would probably leave the same way."[10] Students and faculty rallied to her defense by sending a petition and letters of support to President MacCracken, who promised Millay he would never vote for her expulsion because he didn't "want to have any dead Shelley's on [his] doorstep."[11] Millay was reinstated and allowed to participate in the commencement ceremony, pleased by the show of support on her behalf: "I never knew before that I had so many friends," she wrote to her family. "Everybody is wonderful."[12]

After Vassar, Millay moved to Greenwich Village where she became one of the central figures in a milieu characterized by personal freedom and political radicalism. In 1920, surrounded by other aspiring artists and writers including Eugene O'Neill, Floyd Dell, Djuna Barnes, and Edmund Wilson, Millay was a rising celebrity. With her usual wit and self-deprecating irony, she wrote to Bynner: "I am becoming very famous. The current *Vanity Fair* has a whole page of my poems, and a photograph of me that looks as much like me as it does like Arnold Bennett. And there have been three reviews of something I wrote, in New York newspapers, in the last week alone. I am so incorrigibly ingenuous that these things mean just as much to me as ever. Besides, I just got a prize of a hundred dollars in *Poetry*, for the Beanstalk."[13]

Millay was a free spirit—bohemian in lifestyle, progressive in her convictions about women's rights and social equality, selective in her choice of lovers. Her many suitors, including Dell, Wilson, and John Peale Bishop, considered her an alluring companion but ultimately unattainable life partner. Their published recollections have contributed to Millay's mystique as a woman who both lived and documented the vicissitudes of romantic love.

Indeed, Millay's early poems about love vary widely in feelings and attitudes—from lyrical adulation to deeply felt loss to angry denunciation of the beloved in question. Within the early poems, the most dramatic examples of her own poetic catharsis are the sonnets written for Ficke, who had corresponded with Millay by letter for almost six years when they met for the first time in 1918 in Millay's apartment in New York. A major in the army, Ficke was on a two-day stopover en route to his post in France. He and Millay had a brief, passionate affair before he sailed abroad. Over the next several months, they exchanged letters and love sonnets about the nature—and future—of their relationship. In one of Millay's sonnets written for Ficke, "Into the golden vessel of great song," she proposes that they use their love as inspiration for poetry rather than enjoy commonplace carnality.[14]

While living in New York, Millay enjoyed seeing her poems appear in magazines such as the *Forum*, *Vanity Fair*, and *Ainslee's*, though they brought her little financial reward. She spent some of her time acting in theatrical productions with the Provincetown Players group (also for artistic rather than monetary gain) and in 1919 directed a production of her own *Aria da Capo*, a one-act play that exposes the absurdities of war. To earn a living, she wrote stories—mostly potboiler romances—and satirical sketches under the pen name Nancy Boyd. These prose pieces sometimes appeared in magazines along with poetry signed with Millay's real name. Millay was adamant about keeping her literary reputation separate from that of Nancy Boyd, whose purpose was simply to produce passable writing that would sell. Yet she saw the humor in her situation; in a 1922 letter to her sister Norma, Millay wrote: "Nancy is going strong in *Vanity Fair*, isn't she? Isn't she a blessing? Almost two years now since the woman has been well nigh supporting me."[15] And two years later, when the Nancy Boyd pieces were collected in a book titled *Distressing Dialogues*, the introduction was written by none other than Edna St. Vincent Millay.

Millay attracted a loyal following of readers who, impressed by her talent, verve, and charm, memorized and often imitated her poems. Critics, however, focused on her expertise and development as a poet. Their first accounts were generally positive: Louis Untermeyer exalted *Renascence and Other Poems* (1917) for "an untutored simplicity accompanying an indefinable magic,"[16] and *Vanity Fair* paid the collection compliments for its "naturalness."[17] *A Few Figs from Thistles* (1920) captivated the general audience but garnered a less enthusiastic critical reception. Some reviewers interpreted Millay's ultraconfident, at times cynical, voice favorably as a deliberate facade, a sign of wit or a dramatic technique,[18] while others, who disliked the collection, considered the poems flippant and unpoetic and felt that Millay's use of colloquial language compromised her proven lyrical abilities.

In the influential *New York Times Book Review and Magazine*, William Lyon Phelps wrote that while *Renascence and Other Poems* had revealed Millay's "lyrical gifts" and "vision," *A Few Figs from Thistles* proved she was a typical "child of the twentieth century" who sometimes wrote "in the vein of light cynicism and disillusion . . . [This book] is exceedingly well-named, . . . These whimsies are graceful and amusing enough, but of no importance—not even to their author. A fig for such poetry!"[19] Untermeyer, too, disappointed by the marked change in Millay's tone, described the collection as "a mess of cleverness [reflecting] a facile cynicism."[20]

In January 1921, Millay left New York for Europe under contract as a foreign correspondent to produce two articles a month for *Vanity Fair*. She hoped a change of place and company would give her poetry "fresh grass to feed on"[21] and would restore her health, which had become increasingly uneven. Over the next two years, while visiting Paris, London,

Rome, Vienna, Budapest, and parts of Albania, she wrote magazine pieces, a play, some poetry (including "The Ballad of the Harp-Weaver"), and started a novel, *Hardigut*, which she later abandoned. She also became the center of an intriguing three-way correspondence with Ficke, for whom she continued to express her love and devotion (regardless of the news that he was already engaged), and Bynner, who had fallen in love with her.[22] After a year abroad, Millay's mother joined her and they lived in England and France until Millay's unstable health forced them to return home.

Millay arrived in New York to find that her literary reputation had continued to take shape even in her absence. Reviewers had been writing about her work, in particular her third book, *Second April* (1921), which appealed to a wider and more mature audience of readers than *A Few Figs from Thistles*. They noted that her voice was calmer, more poetic, more serious, and more mature than in the earlier collection; so too her subject matter ventured into darker realms reminiscent of *Renascence and Other Poems*. Most agreed that the volume complemented Millay's auspicious start and gave her high marks for flawless poetic form, emotional depth, and a skillful use of irony.[23]

Indeed, Millay had become one of the most sought-after literary personalities in America: the *New York Times Book Review and Magazine* called her "America's Poet of the Future"[24] and the *Boston Daily Globe* named her one of the most important American women poets.[25] Soon after her return, she was awarded the new but high-profile Pulitzer Prize for Poetry[26] for *A Few Figs from Thistles*, the poem "The Ballad of the Harpweaver," and eight sonnets published in *American Poetry 1922: A Miscellany* (reprinted in 1923 in her next collection, *The Harp-Weaver and Other Poems*[27]).

Yet neither the Pulitzer nor her popularity with the general public won her acceptance by the literati at large. Among the complex reasons for her mixed reception is the particular moment in literary history when she appeared and the fact that male critics viewed her work through a gender-biased lens. Precisely when Millay was expressing attitudes and feelings in (for the most part) conventional poetic forms, other poets—led by Ezra Pound and T. S. Eliot—were expounding a new theory of poetry that rejected the expression of emotion for reliance on the image. The resulting poetic movement, called "modernism," renounced old poetic forms with Pound's instruction to "make it new" and called for, in Eliot's words, the "extinction of personality."[28] Modernist poets, accepting "a heap of broken images"[29] as the central metaphor for contemporary life, wrote in unconventional styles about topics of intellectual interest such as the reintegration of myth in poetry.

The rise of modernism divided both poets and their critical ranks into opposing factions. Those reviewers who favored traditional forms and themes—Untermeyer, Mark Van Doren, Edmund Wilson, and Genevieve Taggard, for example—gave Millay's work high praise, but their modernist counterparts such as Robert Penn Warren, Allen Tate, and John Crowe Ransom considered her work intellectually uninteresting. These critics also categorized Millay as one of the leaders of the "lyrists," a group composed primarily of women, whose lyric poems appeared frequently in popular magazines. This informally assembled group produced structured poetry in the tradition of William Vaughn Moody and Edwin Arlington Robinson; their literary "movement" was, in Amy Lowell's words, "all feminine . . . even in the work of its men."[30]

Most critics considered this popular poetry unworthy of attention. To them, the strong presence of a "feminine sensibility" that defined the poems, manifested by the poet's failure to address metaphysical themes from an emotional distance, rendered the poets lacking in the intellectual component that (to the modernist mind) constituted good literature. For the most part, the lyrists produced carefully chiseled poems, written in strict metrical forms and composed of simple, often "glittering" images that revealed the poet's private thoughts and desires. Much of this writing is similar and predictable in its diction, theme, style, and point of view. But several of the so-called lyrists—Sara Teasdale, Genevieve Taggard, and Elinor Wylie—expanded the scope of their subject matter and style and developed distinctive poetic voices.

Millay, of course, moved far beyond the prescribed boundaries of the lyric genre and took unprecedented risks with her subject matter by favoring women's sexuality as a theme. In doing so she was redefining the culturally accepted idea of "feminine virtue"—an accomplishment that encouraged other women to reevaluate the limitations placed on their lives by their heritage and their society.

The influence of gender on literary criticism is inescapable. Millay's contemporary critics placed her work in a literary context that included the historical male-intellectual / female-emotional dichotomy. Most male modernist critics discussed Millay in terms of that dichotomy, and complained that her writing lacked evidence of intellectual sophistication. Their female counterparts, on the other hand, such as Louise Bogan and Babette Deutsch,[31] were less concerned about whether Millay's poems were intellectually oriented, and concentrated instead on how successfully the poet conveyed her meaning. Interested too in Millay's evolution as a writer, both Bogan and Deutsch examined how her distinctive poetic voice, direct treatment of emotion, and use of traditional form and style worked for or against her purposes. Bogan, for example, in reviewing Millay's successive volumes of poetry, observed that her "maturity" as a writer was hampered by her failure to withdraw her personality from her work. Yet in a retrospective article, she names Millay as one of the women poets who helped revive the spirit of American poetry:

> The cluster of American women poets that appeared on the American scene just before and after 1918 restored genuine and

> frank feelings to a literary situation which had become genteel, artificial and dry. . . . [For example,] Sara Teasdale's later verse [and] the best of Millay's early songs and meditations. . . .[32]

Deutsch, who wrote extensively about Millay, noted that the poet's "modernity" was reflected in her "acknowledgement [in her poems] that the relation between the sexes is not what was painted by the poets of romantic love." Deutsch found Millay's treatment of love in the early poems disappointing because emotion was not conveyed directly but instead through the filter of the archaic "manner" typical of the Cavalier poets. In the "later and more sober love poems" and *Fatal Interview* (1931), Deutsch observed that "the thwartings, the conflicts [of love] . . . [were still] not fully admitted in her verse" because the style was "so archaic." Yet Deutsch continued to regard Millay as an important poet whose poems successfully expressed "the perennial cry against the death of the lover of the sensual world."[33]

The literary climate of the period was problematic in that, with few exceptions, modernism was a male-defined movement. Essentially, this presented women poets with a choice: either write New Poetry—that is, write within a male-defined context and accept a better chance of being endorsed by the male critical establishment—or write in the lyrical mode reminiscent of the nineteenth-century tradition and risk being labeled "derivative" and unintellectual, and therefore unworthy of critical attention. Millay herself acknowledged the gender issues influencing critics, and often spoke out against damaging sexist attitudes and practices within the literary establishment.[34] In the end, her popularity among the general readership lasted regardless of esoteric literary issues or even gender bias.

In 1923, Millay met Eugen Boissevain, a wealthy Dutch importer living in New York, at a weekend house party in Croton-on-Hudson where guests included Ficke and his fiancée and Floyd Dell and his wife.[35] One evening Millay and Boissevain played the title roles in a spoof (composed by Millay and Dell) in which a couple from the city meet on a train to the country and eventually fall in love. As fate would have it, the story became a reality: Millay married Boissevain later that year, and the couple took a honeymoon trip around the world.

In 1925, the couple left Greenwich Village for upstate New York where they bought a berry farm which Millay named Steepletop after the pink-spined wildflower (steeplebush) that grew there. After the long absence from her rural roots in Maine, Millay once again felt close to the natural world, the inspiration for much of her poetry. Steepletop became home base for the poet and her husband; with the exception of summer trips to their small island off the Maine coast, reading tours, and trips abroad, the couple lived there for the rest of their lives.

Within the next decade, Millay published three new poetry collections: *The Buck in the Snow* (1928), *Fatal Interview* (1931), and *Wine from These Grapes* (1934); an opera libretto, *The King's Henchman* (which premiered, with music by Deems Taylor, at the Metropolitan Opera House in New York in 1927[36]); and four plays. In 1936, she also published a translation of Baudelaire's *Flowers of Evil* (which she co-translated from the French with George Dillon[37]). As each of these works compounded the increasingly versatile Millay canon, critics attempting to assign Millay a place in literary history labeled her a Romantic, a Transcendentalist, a classicist, and a poetic descendant of Shakespeare, Donne, Byron, Swinburne, Dickinson, Hardy, and Housman.

In 1937, Millay surprised readers and critics with *Conversation at Midnight*, a verse drama with a cast of seven men from diverse backgrounds: a stockbroker, a painter, a short story writer, a Communist poet, a Catholic priest, an advertising executive, and an agnostic. The men meet in a New York drawing room over drinks and express their opinions about various topics, such as women, politics, and religion, until evening's end. Their dialogue, which becomes more heated and revealing as the night wears on, consists of a collage of poetic styles including sonnets, free verse, and rhyming couplets. Critics responded to both the style and content of *Conversation.* Some expressed dissatisfaction with Millay's shift from timeless themes to contemporary politics; others found the book dull or boring in content and disappointing in poetic impact. The more balanced reviews acknowledged Millay's change of theme as a conscious move and noted the poetic innovations in the work itself. In a rare analogy, one critic compared Millay with Pound and Eliot, noting that she had finally given up "the personal dictatorship of the lyric"[38] to produce poetry with a greater than personal significance.

Millay's next poetry collection, *Huntsman, What Quarry?* (1939), caused little critical stir, as it simply reconfirmed her already acknowledged lyrical abilities. In the 1940s, Millay's literary reputation suffered when she began writing poems for radio broadcasts and for publication that would further the war effort in America. When she shifted her subject matter from nature, love, and personal freedom to politics, her confident and colloquial poetic voice became deadly serious and patriotic, at times high-pitched, in support of the allied cause.

Millay understood the risk to her reputation: in a 1940 letter to George Dillon she wrote of her recently published collection, *Make Bright the Arrows*: "there are a few good poems, but it is mostly plain propaganda."[39] A few months later, she defended her antipacifist stand with the words, "I have one thing to give in the service of my country,—my reputation as a poet."[40] Critics and readers alike were disturbed by this new turn; with the exception of a radio drama in verse, *The Murder of Lidice*,[41] which was received cordially (though unenthusiastically) in 1942, Millay's new work was dismissed as "shoddy and clichéd expression, a singularly disheartening job."[42] Louise Bogan suggested that, regrettably, Millay had regressed to the stock sentiments typical of post–World War I poetry and that such a regression signaled an end to the American poetic renaissance that had begun in 1912.[43]

Millay published no more poetry during her lifetime;[44] after her death in 1950, her sister Norma published selections from her last poems and other unpublished earlier work in *Mine the Harvest* (1954). This volume includes some of Millay's most sophisticated writing: in a range of styles she explores human motivations and desire and confronts the psychological ramifications of her life as a poet. In several poems she attempts to overcome the loneliness she feels after her husband's death (Boissevain died in 1949). The bravado of the early poems noticeably absent, Millay writes in a steadier voice as she berates those critics who dismiss traditional poetry as "tedious, obvious, vacuous, trivial, trite" and reaffirms her allegiance to direct statement by challenging the literary "fashion" of the day that dictates, "Straightforwardness is wrong, evasion right."[45] Also in the collection are twenty sonnets, including a biting defense of traditional form—"I will put Chaos into fourteen lines"—and a series of fragments from her Greenwich Village diaries.[46]

The full story behind Millay's poetic reputation is complex and at times based on speculation, as it is difficult to determine how gender, subject matter, literary quality (itself a relative term), general popularity (indicated by book sales), critical reception, academic acceptance (or rejection), and public image interrelate to create, sustain, or damage a writer's name. What is certain is that today, half a century after Millay's death, her poetry—still popular with the reading public—is finally receiving serious attention from critics, scholars, and editors of literary anthologies. Undoubtedly Millay herself would be pleased, as she had often complained that most editors, not understanding the breadth and seriousness of her work, overlooked some of her best poems.

In the last year of her life she observed that anthologists, "not interested in poetry, interested only in selling their books," always published the same selection of poems because they believed those poems held "the most popular appeal." Millay regretted the reprinting of "such simple and youthful poems as 'Afternoon on a Hill' and 'Recuerdo' " and "only love sonnets, . . . written in the Elizabethan form" rather than a selection which would "be much more interesting, and certainly more representative"[47] of her poetry.

Since then, Millay's reprinted work has included a broader and fairer selection. In the mid-1970s, feminist readers and critics initiated a new wave of Millay scholarship with critical reappraisals of her writing and analyses of her contributions to women's literary and sociocultural history. Subsequent collections of essays about Millay's poems and plays from various critical perspectives have furthered the cause. Clearly, Millay's impact on the American literary tradition far exceeds the confines of the lyrists and the fashionable bravado of the Jazz Age. In the magical way that poetry communicates, her words still appeal not only to readers who enjoy her writing for its lyrical beauty but also to those with more scholarly interests who are forever reading between the lines.

The poems from Millay's first three poetry collections, *Renascence and Other Poems*, *A Few Figs from Thistles*, and *Second April* are included here. This early poetry provides a map that traces a winding path through Millay's literary background and stylistic preferences. Her points of reference and allusions to history, myth, and literature—beginning with her beloved Ovid, Virgil, Catullus, and Petrarch—wend their way into the Renaissance, where her poems rival the songs and sonnets of her favorite mentors—Shakespeare, Sidney, Spenser, Herrick, Marvell, Herbert, and Donne. Like Donne, Millay creates irony and paradox with ingenuity and boldly uses conceits, archaic language, inversions, and complex syntax, adding only twentieth-century colloquial diction as her poetic signature.

Her appreciation of nature's beauty and the joys of rural life, as well as her affinity for the supernatural, echoes the Romantic poets, especially Wordsworth and Coleridge.[48] She identified with the pre-Raphaelite goal of portraying the simplicity of nature and admired Christina Rossetti's lyric gifts. In the poetry of the Brownings and Tennyson, she found metrical excellence and a Victorian sensibility that often suited her; studying the work of other nineteenth-century minds, Emerson and Thoreau, fueled the visionary zeal that eventually ignited "Renascence."

"Renascence" reflects Millay's affinity for Transcendentalism, a nineteenth-century philosophic and literary movement that stressed the unity of all things, the belief that God lives within every human being (thus making "self-reliance" possible), and the notion that every soul is connected to an all-inclusive entity, the World-soul. Ralph Waldo Emerson, spokesperson for the Transcendentalists, defined nature as a fluid element that ascends toward God, with the poet, who was also savior and truth teller, closest to its ascent.[49]

Millay describes this ascent in "Renascence" as her speaker undergoes a terrifying but exhilarating religious experience that changes her conception of the universe.[50] Realizing that her spiritual life is empty, she reaches out with her soul and the world literally caves in on her. In a prolonged moment of revelation, she feels the sin, suffering, and death of everyone in the world, then sinks into the welcome comfort of her grave. Unwilling to leave the earth's beauty behind, she cries out to God and asks to be reborn; her wish is granted and she is miraculously revived: "I know not how such things can be!— / I breathed my soul back into me." Overjoyed, she feels the presence of God's "radiant identity" everywhere, having learned that while the physical world is accessible through thoughts and feelings, the soul is the only vehicle that can move a person closer to God. While "Renascence" may strike contemporary readers as dated or too derivative to be of stylistic or philosophic interest, its timing and positive critical reception assured its importance as both the catalyst for Millay's lifelong career and a milestone in American literary history (it appeared in 1912, the same year Harriet Monroe founded *Poetry: A Magazine of Verse*).

Two other long narrative poems written during the same period, "The Suicide" and "Interim," warrant mention, though neither rivals the technical accomplishment or intellectual appeal of "Renascence." The speaker in "The Suicide" is a young woman who kills herself to escape the trials of life on earth. Arriving in Heaven, her "Father's house," she is initially happy to accept an unscheduled life of pleasantries—music, sun, and sleep. Soon, however, bored with "idleness" and "lonely ease," she appeals to God to give her a task "to dignify [her] days." He refuses, reminding her that she had a task to fulfill—life on earth—and rejected it. As in "Renascence," the protagonist grapples with the meaning of life until she is shown the wisdom of a benevolent but unyielding God. Millay presents a similar theme in "Interim," a first-person account of a man undergoing a spiritual crisis as a result of his wife's recent death. Overwhelmed by grief, he questions his faith in God and cries out for pity, then realizes that "Not Truth, but Faith, it is / That keeps the world alive." Like the speaker in "Renascence," he is spiritually reborn when his shocking revelation leads him back to God.

Replete with exclamations, repetition, and caesuras, the blank verse of "Interim" mirrors the speaker's thought process as he struggles to accept the reality of his loss. Millay's first attempt at writing from a male point of view is not wholly unsuccessful, but the poem falls short of the impressive "Renascence" because of her tendency to overuse conventional poetic devices to convey deep emotion, which never served her as well as the less stylized approach found in shorter lyrics such as "Wild Swans." Also, in "Interim" her overdramatization of familiar images ("You were my flower! / Now let the world grow weeds!") undermines the seriousness and purity of the speaker's situation, diction and word choice at times seem inappropriate to the subject matter ("Amid sensations rendered negative / By your elimination . . ."), and complex syntax occasionally obscures her meaning:

O little words, how can you run so straight
Across the page, beneath the weight you bear?
How can you fall apart, whom such a theme
Has bound together, and hereafter aid
In trivial expression, that have been
So hideously dignified?

"Interim" is ultimately redeemed, in part, by the speaker's tenderness in recalling his wife ("You laughed and brushed your flower against my lips") and in the fresh combination of verbal and visual imagery that aptly describes his mood:

Dark, Dark, is all I find for metaphor;
All else were contrast;—save that contrast's wall
Is down, and all opposed things flow together
Into a vast monotony, where night
And day, and frost and thaw, and death and life,
Are synonyms. . . .

Millay liked this poem; she submitted it to *The Lyric Year* contest along with "Renascence." When she learned "Renascence" had been accepted for publication, she asked the editor to consider publishing "Interim" in its place. He did not, but the following year she found a use for it while taking an English course at Barnard in preparation for Vassar. In May 1913 she wrote to her family:

> I'm feeling awfully tickled about something. . . . Last week, being hard up for a theme to send in, I dug out "Interim" and

> submitted that. I hated to, because Mr. Brewster [William Tenny Brewster, provost at Barnard and professor of English at Columbia] usually reads the verse themes (he picks out three or four themes with a gentle cynicism which would spoil even good verse and is especially hard on middle-class [academic level]. If he takes a dislike to anything he delivers it accordingly & I was scared to death for fear he would read it & I should be obliged to go up and take it away from him).
>
> So this morning, . . . he picked up my "Interim," and I felt a pang. "Gosh," I said to the girl at my right, "I wish he wouldn't read that. He reads verse so *wretchedly*." "Yes, doesn't he?" she agreed, and he began. . . .
>
> He read it beautifully. I was never so astonished in all my life. He had really got hold at last of something he liked, and he was a changed man. He seemed to understand every bit of it. . . .
>
> When he had finished, . . . he [said], "It is a very remarkable production for a girl in college. . . . There are a great number of words here;—a great command of language.—I notice that some of the critics [in the class] say the theme is noticeable for its sincerity. Now it is very obvious that the theme cannot be sincere, since a woman is writing it and a man is supposed to be speaking. It is not sincerity,—it is imagination."
>
> That's about all he said about it, but of course he gave me an A. . . .[51]

Almost all of Millay's early poems are written in traditional forms—the song, the sonnet, the ode, the elegy, and the simple lyric—which she often modified by adjusting a rhyme scheme or revising the meter, adding or dropping beats. Because she often counted stresses instead of syllables to create rhythmic lines and relied judiciously on poetic sound devices such as assonance (*way, bay*), consonance (*stem, them*), alliteration (*singing sweet songs*), and onomatopoeia (*hush*), many of her poems resemble song lyrics: they coax the language to sing.[52] For example, "Recuerdo," composed of rhyming couplets, moves back and forth melodically, driven by the consistency of meter within each stanza and the onomatopoeia created by the repetition of "We were very tired, we were very merry— / We had gone back and forth all night on the ferry." Whether her subject was nature, love, loss, spiritual rebirth, personal freedom, women's sexuality, or the state of the world, Millay was always conscious of how musicality in poetry would help deliver its message.

Nature is Millay's primary source for poetic imagery: nature and its seasons mirror, instruct, and console her and provide a ready context for her various poetic situations and moods. Within the early lyrics are hymns exalting the grandeur of nature, "O world, I cannot hold thee close enough!" ("God's World"); allegories that reveal the impact of its beauty ("The Blue-Flag in the Bog"); and scenes and symbols from its mythology, "Why do you follow me?— / Any moment I can be / Nothing but a laurel-tree" ("Daphne"). In an untitled early poem Millay recalls that her relationship to nature began in childhood: ". . . even then, / [seeing] The grapevine growing over the grey rock—the shock / Of beauty seen, noticed, for the first time— . . . / How did I bear it?"[53] Nature serves as her touchstone for joy—"I will be the gladdest thing / Under the sun! / I will touch a hundred flowers / And not pick one" ("Afternoon on a Hill")—and for sadness—"Sorrow like a ceaseless rain / Beats upon my heart" ("Sorrow").

In "Journey," written in 1913, the poet follows an allegorical path through life, "Following Care along the dusty road," beckoned by the sounds of birds and "creeks at dusk." Anthropomorphizing the forest that awaits her—". . . Eager vines / Go up the rock and wait; flushed apple-trees / Pause in their dance and break the ring for me"—she rejoices in her appreciation of nature's beauty: "The world is mine: blue hill, still silver lake, / Broad field, bright flower, and the long white road." Poetry too assumes a natural form in Millay's imagery scheme—it becomes a bean-stalk that rises high above the sounds and cares of the city and the world, leaving the climber-poet exhausted but joyous: "La, What a climb!" ("The Bean-Stalk").

Like the Romantics, Millay approached nature with religious feeling; seeking consolation for the death of a friend, she is certain the friend's spirit will live on in nature and that "the long year" will remember her ("Mindful of you the sodden earth in spring"). Millay's seasonal imagery ranges from the traditional—a prewinter frost signifies the work of "Death" ("And you as well must die, belovéd dust")—to the unexpected—"Oh, Autumn! Autumn!—What is the Spring to me?" ("The Death of Autumn"). In "Blight," she extends a metaphor based on the "hard seeds of hate" that will not grow properly in the "garden" of her mind. When discouraged by events in the world around her, she bonds with nature, naming herself "Child of all mothers, native of the earth" ("Not in this chamber only at my birth").[54] And when she tires of the noise and bustle of city life, she longs for the beauty and simplicity of a life close to nature in the country ("City Trees") or near the sea ("Eel-Grass," "Inland," "Exiled").

Millay also portrayed the stages of a woman's life with sensitivity and insight. In the early lyrics, she introduced the persona of an adolescent girl living in the country (a situation like that of her own childhood) who feels trapped and lonely but refuses to admit her unhappiness or insecurity. In "Indifference," The Girl[55] waits eagerly for "Love" to come to her at night, but, as the poem's title suggests, she pretends not to care and denies she would go with him (when Love does arrive, however, she is in tears, ready to follow him). In "The Merry Maid," The Girl claims ironically that though her lover left her for another "lass," she has "grown so free from care / Since my heart broke!" In "Travel," she admits that though "the railroad track is miles away," she hears the whistle of every train that passes and vows, ". . . there isn't a train I wouldn't take, / No matter where it's going."

Several of Millay's young women speakers are more savvy and emotionally secure than The Girl; they take great pleasure in defying socially acceptable roles and behavior. These characters range from the young woman in "The Penitent" who revels in being "wicked" rather than pious, to the speaker in "Thursday" who mocks the lover who questions her fickleness, to the raucous young wife in "She Is Overheard Singing" who prefers her roguish, unfaithful husband to the dull, responsible spouses of her five women friends. In rough country dialect, she boasts, "But they all would give the life they live / For a look from the man I kiss!"

In stark contrast to these young women is one of Millay's most realistic and moving characters, the farm wife living in rural New England whose life is defined by her isolation, her relationship with her husband, and the restrictive social conventions associated with her role as a wife.[56] This character is the speaker in two early lyrics that share the same theme: nature's indifference to the human condition. In "Song of a Second April," the speaker observes that nature and the human activity around her proceed exactly as they had the April before, which only deepens her sense of loss and despair at the difference a year has made in her life: "[Now] . . . you are gone, / You that alone I cared to keep." In "Elegy Before Death," a woman anticipating the loss of her husband predicts that the course of nature will be unaffected by his passing—"Spring will not ail nor autumn falter; / Nothing will know that you are gone,—" but that her own perception of nature's beauty will be changed forever:

Oh, there will pass with your great passing
Little of beauty not your own,—
Only the light from common water,
Only the grace from simple stone!

A fitting companion piece for this poem is the sonnet, written in colloquial language, "If I should learn, in some quite casual way," in which the speaker imagines the devastating effect of her lover's death, this time in an urban setting where the landscape consists of subway trains and city streets.

Millay explores the theme of actual loss in "To a Poet that Died Young," commemorating Tennyson,[57] and "Memorial to D. C.," a five-part poem written in memory of Millay's close friend from Vassar, Dorothy Coleman, who died suddenly in 1918, shortly after her graduation from the college. "Memorial" ends with the poet's lament that no sound, however pleasant, can replace the beauty of her friend's voice, not even ". . . the rushing / Of a river underground, / Not the rising of the wind / In the trees before the rain." Yet Millay knows she must face the new, unwelcome silence:

But the music of your talk
Never shall the chemistry
Of the secret earth restore.
All your lovely words are spoken.
Once the ivory box is broken,
Beats the golden bird no more.

Situations and characters from the world of myth and classical literature serve as the basis for allegory in Millay's early poems ("Ode to Silence") or enhance the poet's own commentary on the need for sensuality in the contemporary world ("Doubt No More that Oberon") or illustrate that real lovers face the same temptations as their fictional counterparts ("We talk of taxes, and I call you friend"). In a sonnet entitled "Bluebeard," Millay alludes to a fairy tale about a man who, testing his wife's obedience, gives her a key to a secret chamber that he then forbids her to enter. Defying her husband's orders, the curious wife unlocks the chamber door and, finding the bodies of former wives who had also disobeyed him, knows she will soon meet the same fate. In Millay's sonnet, the poet scolds her lover for trying to pry into her private thoughts and affairs. Her tone is ironic; like Bluebeard's wives, her lover has sealed his own fate. Once he has disturbed her thought process, she abandons it and banishes him in the process: ". . . I must never more behold your face. / This now is yours. I seek another place."[58]

Millay's affinity for fantasy and the supernatural surfaces in the creation of an elusive "Witch-Wife" who ". . . learned her hands on a fairy-tale, / And her mouth on a valentine"; an elegant lady-ghost dressed in white ("The Little Ghost"); and a thin "Wraith" with "glimmering eyes" who haunts her former homestead. Most intriguing, perhaps, is "The Singing-Woman from the Wood's Edge" who brags, "Who should I be but a prophet and a liar, / Whose mother was a leprechaun, whose father was a friar?" This part-human, part-sylvan character first describes, in a lighthearted tone, how she was "born in a bog," "teethed on a crucifix and cradled under water," and brought up with her "playmates . . . the adder and the frog." Though her voice lilts along, her tale darkens as she describes the disorienting result of being raised by parents with opposing values: "After all's said and after all's done, / What should I be but a harlot and a nun?" The woman reveals that her devoutly religious father and sacrilegious mother who "yanked [her] both ways" have left her confused, caught between two distinct personalities that meet—and clash—within her own conflicted self.

Millay modeled this character's situation on her own: the product of incompatible parents, she incorporated opposing worlds—the socially conventional and the radical, the classical and the contemporary. Personally, too, she sought to achieve a balance between the often conflicting forces of body vs. mind, and heart vs. mind.[59] In the singing-woman's case, Millay did not offer a solution to such dilemmas, but she did infuse the character with enough wisdom to accept her fate: "With him for a sire and her for a dam, / What should I be but just what I am?"

In her sonnets, Millay created a composite portrait of a woman in love that represents an unprecedented departure from the traditional portrayal of women in romantic love poetry. Throughout that tradition, consisting primarily of male poets, the speaker typically expresses the pain of longing for the woman he loves, anguish over his rejection as a worthy suitor, or, occasionally, insufferable joy at imagining the ecstasy of their union. The woman he loves (and may address in the poem) is depicted as beautiful, charming, shallow, and apt to act coolly, even cruelly, toward him. Millay contributed generously to this tradition but switched the lovers' gender roles so that the woman would become the speaker.[60] By reversing male-defined poetic conventions and sexual protocols to include female experience, she benefitted from the same paradoxical shift in power that gave the male love poet authority over the woman he pursued: regardless of his lack of success as a suitor, the very act of loving ennobled him and raised his moral stature while the woman functioned merely as a silent object of desire.[61]

Beginning in the early sonnets, Millay's speaker—like her male predecessors—is ostensibly suffering but instead takes center stage. Now *she* is pierced by Cupid's arrow ("Love, though for this you riddle me with darts"), agonizes during her beloved's absence ("Once more into my arid days like dew / . . . the thought of you / Comes to destroy me . . ."), regrets the passing of "unscrupulous Time, / More cruel than Death" that will age her lover ("Oh, my belovèd, have you thought of this"), and mourns the reality that even her love cannot protect him from death ("And you as well must die, belovèd dust").[62] Now she too derives moral stature from being in love by declaring her fidelity to the concept rather than the lover: "Oh, think not I am faithful to a vow! / Faithless I am save to love's self alone" or by dismissing the notion of love altogether for the higher ground of Darwinian theory: "I shall forget you presently, my dear, / . . . / Whether or not we find what we are seeking / Is idle, biologically speaking."

A brilliant verbal strategist, Millay reshapes poetic conventions and strikes rhetorical poses that make her speakers appear either powerful or powerless. In the course of Millay's career, such poses contribute to the evolution of a woman-in-love persona who undergoes rigorous soul searching as she faces the psychological consequences of sexual attraction and desire. She is emotionally vulnerable, motivated not by the desire to manipulate her lover but by the need to express her sexuality, and draws strength from the female elements in nature that comfort her: earth and night. Always, as in the early poems, she is sustained by her devotion to literature and her faith in herself as an artist.

The poems in this volume only partly prepare the reader for the reaches of Millay's later work. Yet they do illustrate her expertise in creating a precarious tension between form and meaning, between neatly sculpted lines and their explosive (or at least unexpected) content.[63] Particularly in the sonnets, form enables Millay to organize and "frame" internal dilemmas and to exert control over the subject in question, usually the lover or love itself. By choosing a subject and then shaping it within the constraints of meter and rhyme, she, the poet, is in charge: she can give a man a time limit for her attentions ("Only until this cigarette is ended") or appoint him as listener to either her musings on sexuality ("Not with libations, but with shouts and laughter") or her pledge of allegiance to a life ruled by immortal art rather than fleeting love ("Cherish you then the hope I shall forget"). The tension that permeates these poems originates, perhaps, from the pressures in Millay's own life, which are sometimes documented but seldom resolved in her writing.

Undoubtedly, the very act of creating poetry empowered her; at the very least it enabled her to impose a measure of order on real and imaginary dilemmas, immobilizing them for closer inspection.[64]

In "The Poet and His Book," Millay entreats future generations, "Read me, do not let me die!" by appealing to a stranger, boys and girls, farmers, shepherds, sailors, scholars, hunters, men, women, and finally a grave digger who may be called upon to bury her but cannot silence her immortal song. Her voice is that of a young poet, dramatic and breathless, trying out a familiar theme, the immortality of art. Yet the plea is heartfelt and resounds with the hope that her poems will both last and be made accessible to a diverse audience.

Time has granted her wish: Millay's poetry has not been forgotten. On the contrary, her books have found their way into thousands of homes, libraries, schools, and universities in the United States and abroad. Millay's place in the American literary tradition, the women's poetry tradition in particular, is still under scrutiny by contemporary scholars because of her distance from modernism and the complexities inherent in her relation to feminism. Yet, clearly, her poetry has a life of its own, creating a vast psychological landscape as the poet shifts her focus from the minutiae of daily life to grand themes with apparent ease. Millay's writing fascinates because it clarifies the human predicament and because it illuminates—though never betrays the secrets of—women's feelings, motivations, and behavior. Perhaps, regardless of our well-meaning efforts to uncover such secrets, it is the relentless "wanting to know" that keeps us reading.

—HOLLY PEPPE
NEW YORK CITY

Notes to the Introduction

1. Lines 1, 7 from the sonnet "To hold secure the Province of Pure Art" in *Edna St. Vincent Millay: Collected Poems*, ed. Norma Millay (New York: Harper & Row, 1956), 723. (Further references to this text will be cited as *CP*.)
2. In 1905, Millay joined the St. Nicholas League, an organization for aspiring writers who could submit their work for publication in the *St. Nicholas* magazine until they reached the age limit of eighteen. Millay, who signed her name "E. St. Vincent Millay," won the top award from the league, the Gold Badge, for "The Land of Romance." In 1907, the poem was reprinted in the literary journal *Current Literature*, with a note from the editor, Edward Wheeler: "The poem which follows seems to me to be phenomenal. The author (whether boy or girl, we do not know) is but fourteen years of age."
3. At the time of *The Lyric Year*'s publication, Ficke was a lawyer living with his wife in Iowa and Bynner, his former classmate at Harvard, was visiting him.
4. *Letters of Edna St. Vincent Millay*, ed. Allan Ross Macdougall (Camden, Maine: Down East Books, 1952), #9. (Further reference to this text will be cited as *Letters*.)
5. Caroline Dow heard Millay perform her work at an evening program for guests at the Whitehall Inn in Camden, Maine, where her sister Norma Millay was working as a waitress over the summer.
6. *Letters*, #14.
7. *Letters*, #38.
8. In 1916, Millay played the medieval poet Marie de France in a pageant honoring women's intellectual achievement. One of the guests in the audience was Inez Milholland—a 1909 Vassar alumna, lawyer, and suffragette leader—who was Millay's role model of an independent woman. In a fittingly poetic twist of fate, Milholland's husband of three years, Eugen Boissevain, would meet and marry his second wife, Millay, seven

years after the two women met at Vassar (Milholland died unexpectedly in late 1916, at age twenty-eight). In 1923, Millay dedicated a sonnet to Milholland (originally entitled "The Pioneer"), which was later published with the title "To Inez Milholland" in *The Buck in the Snow* (1928).

9. Interview with Vassar president emeritus Henry Noble MacCracken (16 November 1966), published in the *Vassarion*, 1967 (Vassar College, Poughkeepsie, New York).

10. *Letters*, #44.

11. Interview with MacCracken (see note #9). Elizabeth Hazelton Haight also tells the story of Millay's near suspension before graduation in her memoir, "Vincent at Vassar," published in the May 1951 issue of *The Vassar Alumnae Magazine* and in pamphlet form later that year.

12. *Letters*, #44.

13. Letter to Witter Bynner (29 October 1920), *Letters*, #74. The poem "The Bean-stalk" was published the following year in *Second April*.

14. In a sonnet sequence written for Millay, Ficke too suggested that their love was ethereal and therefore deserving of artistic rather than earthly consummation. Though Millay wished to marry Ficke (who was in the process of divorcing his wife), he decided later, in 1923, to marry Gladys Brown, an American painter he had met in Paris during the war. Earlier that year, Millay married Eugen Boissevain, an importer from a cultivated, influential Dutch family and they moved to a farmstead in New York State. Soon after, the Fickes moved to a neighboring town. The two couples saw each other regularly and remained friends until Arthur Ficke's death in 1945. For further background on Millay and Ficke's relationship, see Millay's letters to Ficke in *Letters*.

15. *Letters*, #112. Seventeen of Millay's short stories appeared in popular magazines—*Vanity Fair, Ainslee's, The Century Magazine*, and *Metropolitan Magazine*—between 1919 and 1923, ten of them signed with her pen name. Twenty-one satirical

sketches, also signed by Nancy Boyd, were published in *Vanity Fair* between 1921 and 1923 and are collected in *Distressing Dialogues* (New York: Harper and Brothers, 1924). This volume also contains a previously unpublished sketch, "I Like Americans," which was reprinted in *Reader's Digest* in 1938.

16. Louis Untermeyer, *The New Era in American Poetry* (New York: Henry Holt & Co., 1919), 25–26.

17. "Dead Music—An Elegy," *Vanity Fair* 14 (July 1920), 45.

18. Frank Ernest Hill, "Edna St. Vincent Millay," *The Measure* (March 1921), 25–26.

19. William Lyon Phelps, "Edna St. Vincent Millay, Poet and Dramatist," *New York Times Book Review and Magazine* (16 October 1921), 10.

20. Louis Untermeyer, *American Poetry Since 1900* (New York: Henry Holt & Co., 1923), 25–26.

21. *Letters*, #76.

22. This correspondence is truly the "stuff" of poetry, or at least proof that fact is far more intriguing than fiction. In 1921, Bynner proposed marriage to Millay in a letter that was apparently lost in the mail; when Ficke mentioned the proposal to Millay in one of his notes to her (with a postscript from Bynner), Millay wrote Bynner saying that although she never received his formal proposal letter, she would agree to marry him. But that letter crossed in the mail with one from Bynner in which he expressed his "misgivings" about marrying her, given her deep feelings for Ficke. Millay replied to Bynner, declaring, "It is true that I love Arthur. . . . I shall love him always" but assuring Bynner that "I should not wish to marry Arthur, even it were possible,—so it is not because you are free and he is not, Hal, as may have come into your mind." In December of the following year, Millay wrote Ficke: "As for Hal, there's not the slightest danger that I shall marry him: he has jilted me!" (In April, Ficke had arrived in Paris with his fiancée and introduced her to Millay.) All this took an emotional toll on Millay, but she never lost her sense of humor; she ended an emotional

letter to Ficke (in which she admitted she knew, even before being told, that he'd fallen in love with another woman) with the line: "Here's to crime. May the lowliest live to commit it." See *Letters*, #95, 97, 98.

23. Babette Deutsch, "Three Women Poets," *Shadowland* (December 1922), 51.

24. "America's Poet of the Future," *New York Times Book Review and Magazine* (7 August 1921), 2.

25. "Latest Books," *Boston Daily Globe* (6 August 1921), 7.

26. The Pulitzer included a $1000 cash award. Norma Millay was often amused to read accounts that noted, "Millay was the first woman in history to win the Pulitzer Prize for Poetry" when, in fact, Millay was only the second poet to receive the award, which was established in 1922 (Edwin Arlington Robinson was the first winner, Robert Frost the third, in 1924).

27. *The Harp-Weaver and Other Poems* (1923) is arguably Millay's most impressive collection. The title poem is a moving account of a mother's willingness to sacrifice for the son she loves. The thirty-nine sonnets in the volume include some of Millay's most quoted selections—"Pity me not because the light of day," "What lips my lips have kissed, and where, and why"—and an extraordinary sonnet sequence, *Sonnets from an Ungrafted Tree.*

28. T. S. Eliot, "Tradition and the Individual Talent" (1919) in *Selected Prose of T. S. Eliot* (New York: Harcourt Brace & Co., 1975), 40.

29. T. S. Eliot, line 22 from "The Waste Land" (1922) in *The Waste Land and Other Poems* (New York: Harcourt, Brace and World, 1934), 30.

30. Amy Lowell, "Two Generations of American Poetry," *The New Republic* (5 December 1923), 1–3.

31. Babette Deutsch first wrote about Millay's work in 1922 and her subsequent published commentaries trace the poet's career. Even after Millay's death, it was Deutsch who reviewed

her *Collected Poems* and *Collected Sonnets* for the *New York Herald Tribune*. Louise Bogan also wrote about Millay's poetry, beginning in 1935, though not as extensively.

32. Louise Bogan, "The Heart and the Lyre" in *Selected Criticism: Poetry and Prose* (New York: Noonday Press, 1955), 341.

33. Babette Deutsch, *This Modern Poetry* (New York: W. W. Norton & Co., 1935), 99.

34. Millay objected to sexism in the literary world and at large: many of her alliances and actions reflected her support for women's rights and social equality with men. In 1937, for example, Millay registered a complaint with New York University, "not for myself personally, but for all women," upon learning that, as the only woman among those chosen to accept honorary doctoral degrees, she was invited to dine with "a small group of ladies" at the chancellor's house, while the male recipients were invited to dine together at the Waldorf Astoria. See *Letters*, #208.

35. Millay had been introduced to Boissevain, briefly, twice before. Within a month after she met him again in Croton-on-Hudson, she wrote to her mother: "I have been a bad girl not to write to you, . . . But you will forgive me when you know my excuse. Darling, do you remember meeting Eugen Boissevain one day in Waverly Place?—It was only for a moment, & possibly you don't remember. But anyway, you will like him very much, when you know him, which will be soon. And it is important that you should like him,—because I love him very much, & am going to marry him. *There!!!*" (*Letters*, #118).

36. Also in 1927, Millay attracted press attention when, protesting the condemnation of the immigrant anarchists Sacco and Vanzetti, she was arrested and held on bail for taking part in a public demonstration in Boston, then met privately with the governor of Massachusetts to plead for clemency in the case. In "Two Sonnets in Memory," published in *Wine from These Grapes*, Millay registers her anger and disdain toward those who

sealed the immigrants' fate, which she presents metaphorically as the "death" of justice.

37. Millay met George Dillon in 1928 when she read her work at the University of Chicago during a national reading tour. The twenty-two-year-old Dillon, a staff member at *Poetry* magazine, introduced Millay to a large, attentive audience. Their initial meeting sparked a love affair that lasted, on and off, for the next few years. Millay documented her initial passion for Dillon, and its possible detrimental effect on her marriage, in the second sonnet of her fifty-two sonnet sequence *Fatal Interview*: "The scar of this encounter like a sword / Will lie between me and my troubled lord" (lines 13–14). Several of the other poems in the sequence were also evidently written for Dillon. In the end, Millay's marriage long outlasted the affair.

38. Peter Munro Jack, "Conversation of Our Time: Edna St. Vincent Millay's Tapestry of Contemporary Themes," *New York Times Book Review* (25 July 1937), 1. In 1937, another article about Millay appeared that might easily qualify as the locus classicus of gender-based literary criticism: John Crowe Ransom's "The Poet as Woman," published in the *Southern Review* (Spring 1937 issue, pages 783–806). Ransom bases his assessment of Millay's work on the premise that women poets are limited by "the innocent woman mind" and their affinity for emotional rather than intellectual topics; therefore, he concludes, their work is necessarily unintellectual and "inferior" to writing by men. He also postulates that, faced with the combination of woman and poet, a male reviewer will react with ambivalent "attitudes" that make unconditional endorsement (or understanding) of the poet impossible. A testament only to Ransom's own limitations, this article boldly illustrates the dire need for feminist criticism.

39. *Letters*, #309.

40. Letter to Mrs. Charlotte Babcock Sills (2 January 1941), *Letters*, #311.

41. *The Murder of Lidice* is a commemorative poem Millay

wrote at the request of the Writers' War Board for broadcast in the States and by shortwave to England and other countries.

42. Reed Whittemore, "Three Reasons," *Poetry* 90 (April 1957), 52–58.

43. Louise Bogan, review of *Make Bright the Arrows*, *The New Yorker* 16 (28 December 1940), 62.

44. Millay's last published poem, "Thanksgiving . . . 1950," was commissioned by the *Saturday Evening Post* and published in November 1950. See *Letters*, #274.

45. Line 7 from the sonnet "It is the fashion now to wave aside," *CP*, 725.

46. Norma Millay arranged these diary fragments, actually musings in iambic tetrameter, into a "whole" when she edited Millay's *Collected Poems* in 1956. She gave them the title "Journal" for their inclusion in *Mine the Harvest*. Norma Millay, personal interview (23 November 1984).

47. Letter to Bernice Baumgarten (23 June 1950), *Letters*, #273.

48. Millay's Romantic sensibility is reflected in her treatment of nature as a primary subject, her Keatsian attitude toward beauty, and the similarities (in theme and structure) between "Renascence" and *The Rime of the Ancient Mariner*. Her use of neoclassical poetic devices and archaic diction, however, rather than the "language really used by men" disqualifies her as a purist follower of the Romantic movement described by Wordsworth in his preface to *Lyrical Ballads*.

49. The writings of Carlyle, Coleridge, and Wordsworth that reflect the beliefs of the German Transcendentalists greatly influenced Emerson and other members of his Transcendental Club—Henry David Thoreau, Bronson Alcott, Margaret Fuller, and their organizer, Reverend George Ripley. The poetry of Millay's contemporaries Edwin Arlington Robinson and Robert Frost, among others, also reflects Emerson's visionary philosophy interwoven with the Romantics' influence.

50. Soon after Millay and Ficke began corresponding in 1912,

Millay responded to his questions about the origin of "Renascence" (*Letters*, #11):

> If by, "Do you read Coleridge?" you mean, "Is *Renascence* done in imitation of *The Ancient Mariner*—no, it is not. I have read Coleridge, of course; but not for years. And I never even heard of William Blake. (Should I admit it, I wonder?)
>
> As to the line you speak of—"Did you get it from a book? indeed! I'll slap your face. I never get anything from a book. I see things with my own eyes, just as if they were the first eyes that ever saw, and then I set about to tell, as best I can, just what I see.
>
> But I will answer honestly, as you bade me [about whether she experienced the revelation described in the poem]. I did see it, yes. I saw it all, more vividly than you suppose. It was almost an experience. And it is one of the things I don't talk about easily. All of my poems are very real to me, and take a great deal out of me. I am possessed by a masterful and often a cruel imagination.

51. *Letters*, #26.
52. Many of Millay's lyrics and sonnets have been set to music by musicians ranging from instrumentalists to Leonard Bernstein, who set the sonnet "What lips my lips have kissed . . ." (from *The Harp-Weaver and Other Poems*). Millay's one libretto, *The King's Henchman*, was set to music by Deems Taylor.
53. These lines are from an untitled poem first published in 1954 in *Mine the Harvest* (*CP*, 530), which, according to Norma Millay, was written in 1918 when Millay was living in New York City.
54. See "No lack of counsel from the shrewd and wise" (in which she names "my mother the brown earth") and "Night is my sister, and how deep in love," #III and #VII respectively, from *Fatal Interview* (*CP*, 632, 636).
55. Norman Brittin named the adolescent girl persona "The Girl" in one of the first books of scholarly criticism devoted to

Millay's work, *Edna St. Vincent Millay* (Boston: Twayne Publishers, 1982), 35.

56. *Sonnets from an Ungrafted Tree* provides an in-depth profile of one of these lonely women who is barraged by memories and dreams when she returns to take care of the husband she no longer loves. Millay's brilliant portrayal of the wife's unhappiness is intensified by an atmosphere of suspense and spiritual heaviness.

57. Tennyson died at eighty-three; the ironic title of this poem is clarified in lines 17–18: "Here's a song was never sung: / Growing old is dying young." See also the six-part elegy honoring Millay's friend, the poet Elinor Wylie, who died in 1928 (*CP*, 368–375).

58. Millay muses about the "Bluebeard" story at some length in "Journal" (see note #46), clarifying her use of the "locked chamber metaphor" as a reference to the "sealed chamber of [her] mind," which she suspects might be dangerous to visit.

59. Millay pursues these conflicts in depth in her later work. For example, see the sonnet "I, being born a woman and distressed" (*CP*, 601) in which Millay distinguishes women's sexual instincts and attraction from love and warns her admirer against misunderstanding her response to him: "I find this frenzy insufficient reason / For conversation when we meet again." See also "I too beneath your moon, almighty Sex" (*CP*, 688), in which she acknowledges the dichotomy of body and mind from another angle and relates her sexuality to her role as a poet, and "Pity me not because the light of day" (*CP*, 589), which ends: "Pity me that the heart is slow to learn / What the swift mind beholds at every turn." Also of interest here is an intentionally ironic but revealing poem written (according to her friend and *Letters* editor Allan Ross Macdougall) in 1920 when she, John Peale Bishop, and Edmund Wilson were writing self-portraits one evening to amuse themselves. In a letter to Wilson (*Letters*, #72), she asked him "not to circulate" the poem but to "shatter it at once" so it would not

be published in *Vanity Fair.* Her self-portrait (which is published in *Letters,* #72n.) reads:

"E. St. V. M."
Hair which she still devoutly trusts is red.
Colorless eyes, employing
A childish wonder
To which they have no statistic
Title.
A large mouth.
Lascivious,
Aceticized by blasphemies.
A long throat,
Which will someday
Be strangled.
Thin arms,
which in the summer-time leopard
With freckles.
A small body,
Unexclamatory,
But which,
Were it the fashion to wear no clothes,
Would be as well-dressed
As any.

60. Women poets before Millay did use women speakers, but none created as extensive and detailed a portrait of a "woman in love." Among those who wrote love sonnet sequences are Elizabeth Barrett Browning (*Sonnets from the Portuguese*), Christina Rossetti (*Monna Innominata*), and Elinor Wylie (*One Person*), but in each case, a woman speaker stays within the conventional role of the unworthy admirer who lives for her relationship to her lover.
61. This idea originated in the writings of Ovid, the Roman poet (43 B.C.–A.D. 17?) whose *Ars Amatoria* (*The Art of Love*) won high acclaim from the upper-class Roman society of his

day. His work was also highly regarded in the Middle Ages and evolved into the twelfth-century courtly love tradition. For background on the intriguing, albeit misogynous rules defining this tradition, see Andreas Capellanus, *The Art of Courtly Love*, edited and translated by John Jay Perry (New York: W. W. Norton & Co., 1969).

62. These poetic conventions, including carpe diem, the metaphor of love as a jailer or disease, the portrayal of time as the lovers' enemy, and the immortality of poetry vs. the brief human lifespan, are found in abundance in *Fatal Interview*. Donne's influence in particular is easily recognized here, beginning with the title, which is taken from a line in Donne's "Elegie XVI: On His Mistris": "By our first and fatal interview, / By all desires which thereof did ensue, / . . . / I calmly beg . . ."

63. Millay addresses this tension in an extraordinary sonnet, written late in her life, "I will put Chaos into fourteen lines," in which, exerting her control as a poet, she forces the union of "Chaos" and "Order," thereby harnessing the elusive source of the poem's energy (*CP*, 728).

64. Many literary critics have explored issues surrounding how and why poets use poetic form and how form (or the lack of it) affects readers. These issues are particularly absorbing in the case of women poets. In 1931, Genevieve Taggard criticized Millay for using the sonnet form (in *Fatal Interview*) as a means of distancing herself from her feelings, which eventually resulted in the poet's "self-rejection" for the sake of creating literary "perfection" (see "A Woman's Anatomy of Love" in the *New York Herald Tribune Review of Books* [19 April 1931], 3). Addressing the same subject in her essay *When We Dead Awaken* (first published in *College English* in October 1972, 18–25), poet Adrienne Rich recounts that early in her career, she relied on "formalism" as "asbestos gloves," a strategy that "allowed [her] to handle materials [she] couldn't pick up barehanded."

SUGGESTIONS FOR FURTHER READING

BOOKS BY EDNA ST. VINCENT MILLAY (IN CHRONOLOGICAL ORDER)

Poetry

Renascence and Other Poems, 1917.
A Few Figs from Thistles, 1920; expanded ed., 1922.
Second April, 1921.
The Harp-Weaver and Other Poems, 1923.
The Buck in the Snow, 1928.
Edna St. Vincent Millay's Poems Selected for Young People, 1929.
Fatal Interview, 1931.
Wine from These Grapes, 1934.
Conversation at Midnight, 1937.
Huntsman, What Quarry?, 1939.
Make Bright the Arrows, 1940.
Collected Sonnets, 1941; revised and expanded (ed. Elizabeth Barnett), 1988.
The Murder of Lidice, 1942.
Collected Lyrics, 1943.
Mine the Harvest (ed. Norma Millay), 1954.
Collected Poems (ed. Norma Millay), 1956.
The Ballad of the Harp-Weaver; illustrated edition, 1991.
Selected Poems (ed. Colin Falck), 1991; U.K. edition, 1992.

Prose

Distressing Dialogues (under pseudonym Nancy Boyd), 1924.

Plays

Aria da Capo, 1920.

The Lamp and the Bell, 1921.

Two Slatterns and a King, 1921.

The King's Henchman (opera libretto), 1927.

The Princess Marries the Page, 1932.

Translations

Flowers of Evil, from the French of Charles Baudelaire (with George Dillon), 1936.

Letters

Letters of Edna St. Vincent Millay (ed. Allan Ross Macdougall), 1952.

SECONDARY SOURCES

Books

Abrams, M. H., E. Talbot Donaldson, Hallett Smith, Robert M. Adams, Samuel Holt Monk, George H. Ford, and David Daiches, eds. *The Norton Anthology of English Literature*, vols. I and II. New York: W. W. Norton & Co., 1968.

Baker, Hershel, ed. *The Later Renaissance in England: Nondramatic Verse and Prose, 1600–1660.* Boston: Houghton Mifflin Co., 1975.

Benet, William Rose. *The Reader's Encyclopedia.* New York: Thomas Y. Crowell Co., 1965.

Bloom, Harold. *The Anxiety of Influence: A Theory of Poetry.* New York: Oxford University Press, 1973.

Bogan, Louise. *Achievement in American Poetry, 1900–1950.* Chicago: H. Regnery Co., 1951.

———. "The Heart and the Lyre" in *Selected Criticism: Poetry and Prose*, 335–42. New York: Noonday Press, 1955.

Braithwaite, William Stanley Beaumont. *Anthology of Magazine Verse, 1912–1930.* New York: G. Sully & Co., 1929.

Brittin, Norman A. *Edna St. Vincent Millay*. Rev. ed. Boston: G. K. Hall & Co., 1982.

Brooks, Cleanth, R. W. B. Lewis, and Robert Penn Warren, eds. *American Literature: The Makers and the Making*, vols. I and II. New York: St. Martin's Press, 1973.

Capellanus, Andreas. *The Art of Courtly Love*. Ed. and trans. by John Jay Perry. New York: W. W. Norton & Co., 1969.

Churchill, Allen. *The Improper Bohemians*. New York: E. P. Dutton Co., 1959.

Cook, Harold Lewis. "Edna St. Vincent Millay,—An Essay" in *A Bibliography of the Works of Edna St. Vincent Millay*, ed. Karl Yost, 7–55. New York: Harper & Brothers, 1937.

Cowley, Malcolm. *—And I Worked at the Writer's Trade: Chapters of Literary History, 1918–1978*. New York: Penguin Books, 1979.

———. "Postscript: Twenty Years of American Literature" in *After the Genteel Tradition: American Writers Since 1910*, ed. Malcolm Cowley, 213–34. New York: W. W. Norton & Co., 1937.

Daffron, Carolyn. *Edna St. Vincent Millay* (American Women of Achievement series). New York: Chelsea House, 1989.

D'Aulaire, Ingri, and Edgar D'Aulaire. *D'Aulaires' Book of Greek Myths*. New York: Doubleday & Co., 1962.

Dell, Floyd. *Homecoming: An Autobiography*. New York: Farrar, Straus & Cudahy, 1959.

———. *Love in Greenwich Village*. New York: George H. Doran & Co., 1926.

Deutsch, Babette. *Poetry in Our Time*. New York: Columbia University Press, 1956.

———. *This Modern Poetry*. New York: W. W. Norton & Co., 1935.

Diggory, Terence. "Armoured Women, Naked Men" in *Shakespeare's Sisters: Feminist Essays on Women Poets*, ed. Sandra M. Gilbert and Susan Gubar, 135–52. Bloomington: Indiana University Press, 1979.

Eastman, Max. "My Friendship with Edna Millay" in *Great Companions: Critical Memoirs of Some Famous Friends*, 77–104. New York: Farrar, Straus & Cudahy, 1959.

Eliot, T. S. "Tradition and the Individual Talent" in *Selected Prose of T. S. Eliot*, ed. Frank Kermode, 37–44. New York: Harcourt Brace & Co., 1975.

Farr, Judith. "Elinor Wylie, Edna St. Vincent Millay, and the Elizabethan Sonnet Tradition" in *Poetic Traditions of the English Renaissance*, eds. Maynard Mack and George deForest Lord, 287–305. New Haven: Yale University Press, 1982.

Ficke, Arthur Davison. "Epitaph for the Poet V [Hymn to Intellectual Beauty] to Edna St. Vincent Millay" in *Sonnets of a Portrait Painter*, 89–105. New York: Mitchell Kennerly, 1922.

Freedman, Diane, ed. *Millay at 100: A Critical Reappraisal*. Carbondale: Southern Illinois University Press, 1995.

Gilbert, Sandra M., and Susan Gubar, eds. *The Norton Anthology of Literature by Women*. New York: W. W. Norton & Co., 1985.

Gottesman, Ronald, Laurence B. Holland, David Kalstone, Francis Murphy, Hershel Parker, and William H. Pritchard, eds. *The Norton Anthology of American Literature*. New York: W. W. Norton & Co., 1979.

Gould, Jean. *The Poet and Her Book: A Biography of Edna St. Vincent Millay*. New York: Dodd, Mead & Co., 1969.

Graves, Robert. *The Greek Myths*, vol. I. Baltimore: Penguin Books, 1955.

Gray, James. *Edna St. Vincent Millay*. University of Minnesota Pamphlets on American Writers, #64. Minneapolis: University of Minnesota Press, 1967.

Gurko, Miriam. *Restless Spirit: The Life of Edna St. Vincent Millay*. New York: Thomas Y. Crowell Co., 1962.

Jobes, Gertrude. *Dictionary of Mythology, Folklore and Symbols*, vols. I and II. New York: Scarecrow Press, 1962.

Kenner, Hugh. *The Pound Era.* Berkeley: University of California Press, 1971.

Kreymborg, Alfred. *Our Singing Strength: An Outline of American Poetry, 1620–1930.* New York: Coward McCann, Inc., 1929.

MacCracken, Henry Noble. *The Hickory Limb.* New York: Charles Scribner's Sons, 1950.

Macdougall, Allan Ross, ed. *Letters of Edna St. Vincent Millay.* Camden, Maine: Down East Books, 1952.

Martindale, Charles, ed. *The Cambridge Companion to Virgil.* New York: Cambridge University Press, 1997.

Sheehan, Vincent. *Indigo Bunting: A Memoir of Edna St. Vincent Millay.* New York: Harper & Brothers, 1951.

Taylor, Deems. "Edna St. Vincent Millay, 1892–1950" in *Commemorative Tributes of the American Academy of Arts and Letters, 1942–1951*, 103–108. New York: The American Academy of Arts and Letters, 1951.

Thesing, William B., ed. *Critical Essays on Edna St. Vincent Millay.* New York: G. K. Hall & Co., 1993.

Untermeyer, Louis. *American Poetry Since 1900.* New York: Henry Holt & Co., 1923.

———. *The New Era in American Poetry.* New York: Henry Holt & Co., 1919.

Van Doren, Carl. "Youth and Wings: Edna St. Vincent Millay" in *Many Minds: Critical Essays on American Writers*, 105–19. New York: Alfred A. Knopf, 1924.

Van Doren, Carl, and Mark Van Doren. "Edna St. Vincent Millay" in *American and British Literature Since 1890*, 38–45. New York: Century, 1925.

Walker, Cheryl. *Masks Outrageous and Austere: Culture, Psyche, and Persona in Modern Women Poets.* Bloomington: Indiana University Press, 1991.

Wilson, Edmund. *Letters on Literature and Politics, 1912–1972*, ed. Elena Wilson, 66–72. New York: Farrar, Straus & Giroux, 1977.

———. *The Shores of Light: A Literary Chronicle of the Twenties and Thirties.* New York: Farrar, Straus & Young, 1952; reprint, New York: Vintage Books, 1961.

Wood, Clement. "Edna St. Vincent Millay: A Clever Sappho" in *Poets of America*, 199–213. New York: E. P. Dutton, 1925.

Periodicals, Commentaries, Dissertations

"America's Poet of the Future." *The New York Times Book Review and Magazine* (7 August 1921): 2.

Barnett, Elizabeth, ed. *Tamarack: Journal of the Edna St. Vincent Millay Society.* Vols I–III (Spring 1981; Winter 1982–1983; Fall 1985–Winter 1986).

Bogan, Louise. "Conversion into Self." *Poetry* 45 (February 1935): 277–79.

———. "From the Journals of a Poet." *The New Yorker* 50 (30 January 1978): 39–42, 47–50, 57–58, 63, 66–70.

———. Review of *Make Bright the Arrows. The New Yorker* 16 (28 December 1940): 62.

———. "Verse." *The New Yorker* 15 (20 May 1939): 80–82.

Bynner, Witter. "Edna St. Vincent Millay." *New Republic* 41 (December 1924): 14–15.

Ciardi, John. "Edna St. Vincent Millay: A Figure of Passionate Living." *Saturday Review of Literature* 33 (11 November 1950): 8–9, 77.

"Dead Music—An Elegy." *Vanity Fair* 14 (July 1920): 45.

Dell, Floyd. "Edna St. Vincent Millay." *The Bookman* 56 (January 1922): 272–78.

Deutsch, Babette. "Alas!" *New Republic* 56 (7 November 1928): 333–34.

———. "Lady After Fox." *The Nation* 148 (27 May 1939): 618.

———. "Mme. Jeremiah." *New Republic* 103 (2 December 1940): 761.

———. Review of *Collected Lyrics. New York Herald Tribune* (28 June 1959): 10.

———. Review of *Collected Sonnets. New York Herald Tribune* (28 June 1959): 10.

———. "Three Women Poets." *Shadowland* 7 (December 1922): 51, 71, 75.

———. "Yankee Prophetess." *Saturday Review of Literature* 35 (15 November 1952): 26.

Dobbs, Jeannine. "Edna St. Vincent Millay and the Tradition of Domestic Poetry." *Journal of Women's Studies in Literature* 1 (1979): 89–106.

Gassman, Janet. "Edna St. Vincent Millay: 'Nobody's Own.' " *Colby Library Quarterly* 9 (June 1971): 297–310.

Haight, Elizabeth Hazelton. "Vincent at Vassar." *Vassar Alumnae Magazine* (May 1951): 1–6.

Hill, Frank Ernest. "Edna St. Vincent Millay." *The Measure,* no. 1 (March 1921): 25–26.

Hutchens, John K. "Miss Millay's New Poem: 'The Murder of Lidice' Has Its First Radio Hearing, and Shapes Crime into a Symbol for All the World to Heed." *The New York Times* (25 October 1942) section 8: 12.

Jack, Peter Monro. "Conversation of Our Time: Edna St. Vincent Millay's Tapestry of Contemporary Themes." *The New York Times Book Review* (25 July 1937): 1, 12.

"Latest Books." *Boston Daily Globe* (6 August 1921): 7.

Lowell, Amy. "Two Generations in American Poetry." *New Republic* 37 (5 December 1923) supplement: 1–3.

MacCracken, Henry Noble. Interview at Vassar College, Poughkeepsie, New York (16 November 1966), published in *The Vassarion* (1967): 51–55.

Monroe, Harriet. "Advance or Retreat?" *Poetry* 38 (July 1931): 216–21.

———. "Edna St. Vincent Millay." *Poetry* 24 (August 1924): 260–66.

———. "First Books of Verse." *Poetry* 13 (December 1918): 167–68.

———. "Miss Millay's New Book." *Poetry* 33 (January 1929): 210–14.

Patton, John. "Edna St. Vincent Millay as a Verse Dramatist." Dissertation, University of Colorado, 1962.

———. "Satiric Fiction in Millay's *Distressing Dialogues*." *Modern Language Studies* 2 (Summer 1972): 63–67.

Peppe, Holly. "Rewriting the Myth of the Woman in Love: Edna St. Vincent Millay, Her Critics and Her Sonnets." Dissertation, University of New Hampshire, 1987.

Phelps, William Lyon. "Edna St. Vincent Millay, Poet and Dramatist." *The New York Times Book Review and Magazine* (16 October 1921): 10.

Ransom, John Crowe. "The Poet as Woman." *Southern Review* 2 (Spring 1937): 783–806.

Rich, Adrienne. "When We Dead Awaken: Writing as Re-Vision." *College English* XXXIV, 1 (October 1972): 18–25.

Scott, Winifred Townley. "A Handful of Living Flowers." *Saturday Review of Literature* 40 (5 January 1957): 18–19.

———. "Millay Collected." *Poetry* 63 (March 1944): 334–42.

Taggard, Genevieve. "A Woman's Anatomy of Love." *New York Herald Tribune Review of Books* (19 April 1931): 3.

———. "Classics of the Future." *American Review* (November–December 1924): 620–630.

———. "Her Massive Sandal." *The Measure* 38 (April 1924): 11–16.

Untermeyer, Louis. "Seven Men Talking." *Saturday Review of Literature* 16 (24 July 1937): 6.

———. "Songs from Thistles." *Saturday Review of Literature* 5 (13 October 1928): 209.

———. "Why a Poet Should Never Be Educated." *The Dial* 64 (14 February 1918): 145–47.

Whipple, Leon. Review of *The Murder of Lidice*. *Survey Graphic* 31 (December 1942): 599.

Whittemore, Reed. "Three Reasons." *Poetry* 90 (April 1957): 52–58.

Wilson, Edmund. "Edna St. Vincent Millay: A Memoir." *The Nation* 174 (19 April 1952), 370–83. Reprinted in revised form as "Epilogue, 1952: Edna St. Vincent Millay" in *The Shores of Light*, 229–47.

Bibliographies

Keys, Kay Elaine. "Edna St. Vincent Millay: A Descriptive Bibliography." Dissertation, University of Texas at Austin, 1978.

Nierman, Judith. *Edna St. Vincent Millay: A Reference Guide.* Boston: G. K. Hall & Co., 1977.

Nierman, Judith, and John Patton. "Annotated Bibliography of Works About Edna St. Vincent Millay, 1974–1993" (plus supplement for 1912–1973). University of Maryland Women's Studies, 1997. Available on the Internet at: http:/www.inform.umd.edu:8080/LdRes/Topic/Womens Studies/Bibliographies/Millay

Yost, Karl. *A Bibliography of the Works of Edna St. Vincent Millay.* New York: Harper & Brothers, 1937.

A NOTE ON THE TEXT

The text presented here consists of Millay's first three volumes of poetry: *Renascence and Other Poems* (1917); *A Few Figs from Thistles* (1920; expanded version, 1922); and *Second April* (1921). All of the poems except "The Prisoner" (reprinted here from *A Few Figs from Thistles*) appear in *Collected Poems* (1956), edited by Norma Millay, which is cited throughout the text as *CP* followed by the page number. The sonnets alone are reprinted in *Collected Sonnets*, first published by Millay in 1941 and later published in a revised and expanded edition in 1988 with a preface by Elizabeth Barnett and an introduction by Norma Millay. In Millay's foreword (which appears in both editions), she explains that "through oversight," the sonnet "I do but ask that you be always fair" was published "in magazine form" but had not appeared in any of her books. She added it to that collection as the first sonnet in the *A Few Figs* section, where it remains (in the original edition of *A Few Figs*, sonnets were grouped under the title "Four Sonnets").

In this edition, as in all previous collections and in Millay's original volumes, poems divided into numbered sections (such as "Three Songs of Shattering") are designated with Roman rather than Arabic numerals. The five-part "Memorial to D. C." was first printed in *Second April* with titles designating each section; in *Collected Lyrics*, Millay added Roman numerals above each title and switched the order of the last two sections, which is how it appears here.

To facilitate referencing particular sonnets from various volumes, and in accordance with the 1988 edition of *Collected Sonnets*, only sonnets that are part of a sonnet sequence are numbered. (Because all the early sonnets reprinted in this volume are individual, none are numbered but may be referenced instead by first line.)

The order of the poems here follows that of the three original volumes, with the sonnets placed after the lyrics in their respective collections (unlike *Collected Poems*, in which all the lyrics from different books appear together, followed by all the sonnets). To be consistent, however, and in accordance with *Collected Lyrics* and *Collected Poems*, "Wild Swans" has been placed as the last poem in the lyrics section of *Second April* rather than as the last poem in the volume (after the sonnets), as in the original collection.

Poems are indexed by first line and by title; sonnets are alphabetized by first line. Notes to the poems are numbered consecutively within each of the three volumes and appear at the end of the book. Throughout the text, Millay's use of English (rather than American) spelling has been retained. Punctuation and spelling are based upon Millay's revisions (made from the original texts) that appear in *Collected Lyrics* (1943) and are reprinted accordingly in *Collected Poems* and *Collected Sonnets*.

All excerpts from Millay's letters are taken from Allan Ross Macdougall, ed., *Letters of Edna St. Vincent Millay* (Camden, Maine: Down East Books, 1952) and are cited as *Letters* followed by the letter number.

EARLY POEMS

RENASCENCE

AND

OTHER POEMS

RENASCENCE[1]

All I could see from where I stood
Was three long mountains and a wood;
I turned and looked another way,[2]
And saw three islands in a bay.
So with my eyes I traced the line
Of the horizon, thin and fine,
Straight around till I was come
Back to where I'd started from;
And all I saw from where I stood
Was three long mountains and a wood.

Over these things I could not see:
These were the things that bounded me.
And I could touch them with my hand,
Almost, I thought, from where I stand!
And all at once things seemed so small
My breath came short, and scarce at all.
But, sure, the sky is big, I said:
Miles and miles above my head.
So here upon my back I'll lie
And look my fill into the sky.
And so I looked, and after all,
The sky was not so very tall.
The sky, I said, must somewhere stop . . .
And—sure enough!—I see the top!
The sky, I thought, is not so grand;
I 'most could touch it with my hand!

And reaching up my hand to try,
I screamed, to feel it touch the sky.

I screamed, and—lo!—Infinity
Came down and settled over me;
Forced back my scream into my chest;
Bent back my arm upon my breast;
And, pressing of the Undefined
The definition on my mind,
Held up before my eyes a glass
Through which my shrinking sight did pass
Until it seemed I must behold
Immensity made manifold;
Whispered to me a word whose sound
Deafened the air for worlds around,
And brought unmuffled to my ears
The gossiping of friendly spheres,
The creaking of the tented sky,
The ticking of Eternity.

I saw and heard, and knew at last
The How and Why of all things, past,
And present, and forevermore.
The Universe, cleft to the core,
Lay open to my probing sense,
That, sickening, I would fain pluck thence
But could not,—nay! but needs must suck
At the great wound, and could not pluck
My lips away till I had drawn
All venom out.—Ah, fearful pawn:
For my omniscience paid I toll
In infinite remorse of soul.

All sin was of my sinning, all
Atoning mine, and mine the gall
Of all regret. Mine was the weight
Of every brooded wrong, the hate
That stood behind each envious thrust,
Mine every greed, mine every lust.

And all the while, for every grief,
Each suffering, I craved relief
With individual desire;
Craved all in vain! And felt fierce fire
About a thousand people crawl;
Perished with each,—then mourned for all!

A man was starving in Capri;
He moved his eyes and looked at me;
I felt his gaze, I heard his moan,
And knew his hunger as my own.

I saw at sea a great fog bank
Between two ships that struck and sank;
A thousand screams the heavens smote;
And every scream tore through my throat.

No hurt I did not feel, no death
That was not mine; mine each last breath
That, crying, met an answering cry
From the compassion that was I.
All suffering mine, and mine its rod;
Mine, pity like the pity of God.

Ah, awful weight! Infinity
Pressed down upon the finite Me!

My anguished spirit, like a bird,
Beating against my lips I heard;
Yet lay the weight so close about
There was no room for it without.
And so beneath the weight lay I
And suffered death, but could not die.

Long had I lain thus, craving death,
When quietly the earth beneath
Gave way, and inch by inch, so great
At last had grown the crushing weight,
Into the earth I sank till I
Full six feet under ground did lie,
And sank no more,—there is no weight
Can follow here, however great.
From off my breast I felt it roll,
And as it went my tortured soul
Burst forth and fled in such a gust
That all about me swirled the dust.

Deep in the earth I rested now.
Cool is its hand upon the brow
And soft its breast beneath the head
Of one who is so gladly dead.
And all at once, and over all
The pitying rain began to fall;[3]
I lay and heard each pattering hoof
Upon my lowly, thatchèd roof,
And seemed to love the sound far more
Than ever I had done before.
For rain it hath a friendly sound
To one who's six feet under ground;

And scarce the friendly voice or face,
A grave is such a quiet place.[4]

The rain, I said, is kind to come
And speak to me in my new home.
I would I were alive again
To kiss the fingers of the rain,
To drink into my eyes the shine
Of every slanting silver line,
To catch the freshened, fragrant breeze
From drenched and dripping apple-trees.
For soon the shower will be done,
And then the broad face of the sun
Will laugh above the rain-soaked earth
Until the world with answering mirth
Shakes joyously, and each round drop
Rolls, twinkling, from its grass-blade top.

How can I bear it, buried here,
While overhead the sky grows clear
And blue again after the storm?
O, multi-coloured, multi-form,
Belovèd beauty over me,
That I shall never, never see
Again! Spring-silver, autumn-gold,
That I shall never more behold!—
Sleeping your myriad magics through,
Close-sepulchred away from you!
O God, I cried, give me new birth,
And put me back upon the earth!
Upset each cloud's gigantic gourd
And let the heavy rain, down-poured

In one big torrent, set me free,
Washing my grave away from me!

I ceased; and through the breathless hush
That answered me, the far-off rush
Of herald wings came whispering
Like music down the vibrant string
Of my ascending prayer, and—crash!
Before the wild wind's whistling lash
The startled storm-clouds reared on high
And plunged in terror down the sky!
And the big rain in one black wave
Fell from the sky and struck my grave.

I know not how such things can be;
I only know there came to me
A fragrance such as never clings
To aught save happy living things;
A sound as of some joyous elf
Singing sweet songs to please himself,
And, through and over everything,
A sense of glad awakening.
The grass, a-tiptoe at my ear,
Whispering to me I could hear;
I felt the rain's cool finger-tips
Brushed tenderly across my lips,
Laid gently on my sealèd sight,
And all at once the heavy night
Fell from my eyes and I could see!—
A drenched and dripping apple-tree,
A last long line of silver rain,
A sky grown clear and blue again.
And as I looked a quickening gust

Of wind blew up to me and thrust
Into my face a miracle
Of orchard-breath, and with the smell,—
I know not how such things can be!—
I breathed my soul back into me.

Ah! Up then from the ground sprang I
And hailed the earth with such a cry
As is not heard save from a man
Who has been dead, and lives again.
About the trees my arms I wound;
Like one gone mad I hugged the ground;
I raised my quivering arms on high;
I laughed and laughed into the sky;
Till at my throat a strangling sob
Caught fiercely, and a great heart-throb
Sent instant tears into my eyes:
O God, I cried, no dark disguise
Can e'er hereafter hide from me
Thy radiant identity!
Thou canst not move across the grass
But my quick eyes will see Thee pass,
Nor speak, however silently,
But my hushed voice will answer Thee.
I know the path that tells Thy way
Through the cool eve of every day;
God, I can push the grass apart
And lay my finger on Thy heart!

The world stands out on either side
No wider than the heart is wide;
Above the world is stretched the sky,—
No higher than the soul is high.

The heart can push the sea and land
Farther away on either hand;
The soul can split the sky in two,
And let the face of God shine through.
But East and West will pinch the heart
That can not keep them pushed apart;
And he whose soul is flat—the sky
Will cave in on him by and by.

INTERIM[5]

The room is full of you!—As I came in
And closed the door behind me, all at once
A something in the air, intangible,
Yet stiff with meaning, struck my senses sick!—

Sharp, unfamiliar odours have destroyed
Each other room's dear personality.
The heavy scent of damp, funeral flowers,—
The very essence, hush-distilled, of Death—
Has strangled that habitual breath of home
Whose expiration leaves all houses dead;
And wheresoe'er I look is hideous change.
Save here. Here 'twas as if a weed-choked gate
Had opened at my touch, and I had stepped
Into some long-forgot, enchanted, strange,
Sweet garden of a thousand years ago
And suddenly thought, "I have been here before!"

You are not here. I know that you are gone,
And will not ever enter here again.
And yet it seems to me, if I should speak,
Your silent step must wake across the hall;
If I should turn my head, that your sweet eyes
Would kiss me from the door.—So short a time
To teach my life its transposition to
This difficult and unaccustomed key!—

The room is as you left it; your last touch—
A thoughtless pressure, knowing not itself
As saintly—hallows now each simple thing;
Hallows and glorifies, and glows between
The dust's grey fingers like a shielded light.

There is your book, just as you laid it down,
Face to the table,—I cannot believe
That you are gone!—Just then it seemed to me
You must be here. I almost laughed to think
How like reality the dream had been;
Yet knew before I laughed, and so was still.
That book, outspread, just as you laid it down!
Perhaps you thought, "I wonder what comes next,
And whether this or this will be the end";
So rose, and left it, thinking to return.
Perhaps that chair, when you arose and passed
Out of the room, rocked silently a while
Ere it again was still. When you were gone
Forever from the room, perhaps that chair,
Stirred by your movement, rocked a little while,
Silently, to and fro . . .

And here are the last words your fingers wrote,
Scrawled in broad characters across a page
In this brown book I gave you. Here your hand,
Guiding your rapid pen, moved up and down.
Here with a looping knot you crossed a "t,"
And here another like it, just beyond
These two eccentric "e's." You were so small,
And wrote so brave a hand!
How strange it seems
That of all words these are the words you chose!

And yet a simple choice; you did not know
You would not write again. If you had known—
But then, it does not matter,—and indeed
If you had known there was so little time
You would have dropped your pen and come to me
And this page would be empty, and some phrase
Other than this would hold my wonder now.
Yet, since you could not know, and it befell
That these are the last words your fingers wrote,
There is a dignity some might not see
In this, "I picked the first sweet-pea today."
Today! Was there an opening bud beside it
You left until tomorrow?—O my love,
The things that withered,—and you came not back!
That day you filled this circle of my arms
That now is empty. (O my empty life!)
That day—that day you picked the first sweet-pea,—
And brought it in to show me! I recall
With terrible distinctness how the smell
Of your cool gardens drifted in with you.
I know, you held it up for me to see
And flushed because I looked not at the flower,
But at your face; and when behind my look
You saw such unmistakable intent
You laughed and brushed your flower against my lips.
(You were the fairest thing God ever made,
I think.) And then your hands above my heart
Drew down its stem into a fastening,
And while your head was bent I kissed your hair.
I wonder if you knew. (Belovèd hands!
Somehow I cannot seem to see them still.
Somehow I cannot seem to see the dust
In your bright hair.) What is the need of Heaven

When earth can be so sweet?—If only God
Had let us love,—and show the world the way!
Strange cancellings must ink the eternal books
When love-crossed-out will bring the answer right!

That first sweet-pea! I wonder where it is.
It seems to me I laid it down somewhere,
And yet,—I am not sure. I am not sure,
Even, if it was white or pink; for then
'Twas much like any other flower to me,
Save that it was the first. I did not know,
Then, that it was the last. If I had known—
But then, it does not matter. Strange how few,
After all's said and done, the things that are
Of moment.
Few indeed! When I can make
Of ten small words a rope to hang the world!
"I had you and I have you now no more."
There, there it dangles,—where's the little truth
That can for long keep footing under that
When its slack syllables tighten to a thought?
Here, let me write it down! I wish to see
Just how a thing like that will look on paper!

"I had you and I have you now no more."

O little words, how can you run so straight
Across the page, beneath the weight you bear?
How can you fall apart, whom such a theme
Has bound together, and hereafter aid
In trivial expression, that have been
So hideously dignified?

Would God
That tearing you apart would tear the thread
I strung you on! Would God—O God, my mind
Stretches asunder on this merciless rack
Of imagery! Oh, let me sleep a while!
Would I could sleep, and wake to find me back
In that sweet summer afternoon with you.
Summer? 'Tis summer still by the calendar!
How easily could God, if He so willed,
Set back the world a little turn or two!—
Correct its griefs, and bring its joys again!

We were so wholly one I had not thought
That we could die apart. I had not thought
That I could move,—and you be stiff and still!
That I could speak,—and you perforce be dumb!
I think our heart-strings were, like warp and woof
In some firm fabric, woven in and out;
Your golden filaments in fair design
Across my duller fibre. And today
The shining strip is rent; the exquisite
Fine pattern is destroyed; part of your heart
Aches in my breast; part of my heart lies chilled
In the damp earth with you. I have been torn
In two, and suffer for the rest of me.
What is my life to me? And what am I
To life,—a ship whose star has guttered out?
A Fear that in the deep night starts awake
Perpetually, to find its senses strained
Against the taut strings of the quivering air,
Awaiting the return of some dread chord?

Dark, Dark, is all I find for metaphor;
All else were contrast;—save that contrast's wall
Is down, and all opposed things flow together
Into a vast monotony, where night
And day, and frost and thaw, and death and life,
Are synonyms. What now—what now to me
Are all the jabbering birds and foolish flowers
That clutter up the world? You were my song!
Now, now, let discord scream! You were my flower!
Now let the world grow weeds! For I shall not
Plant things above your grave—(the common balm
Of the conventional woe for its own wound!)
Amid sensations rendered negative
By your elimination stands today,
Certain, unmixed, the element of grief;
I sorrow; and I shall not mock my truth
With travesties of suffering, nor seek
To effigy its incorporeal bulk
In little wry-faced images of woe.
I cannot call you back; and I desire
No utterance of my immaterial voice.
I cannot even turn my face this way
Or that, and say, "My face is turned to you";
I know not where you are, I do not know
If heaven hold you or if earth transmute,
Body and soul, you into earth again;
But this I know:—not for one second's space
Shall I insult my sight with visionings
Such as the credulous crowd so eager-eyed
Beholds, self-conjured in the empty air.
Let the world wail! Let drip its easy tears!
My sorrow shall be dumb!

—What do I say?
God! God!—God pity me! Am I gone mad
That I should spit upon a rosary?
Am I become so shrunken? Would to God
I too might feel that frenzied faith whose touch
Makes temporal the most enduring grief;
Though it must walk a while, as is its wont,
With wild lamenting! Would I too might weep
Where weeps the world and hangs its piteous wreaths
For its new dead! Not Truth, but Faith, it is
That keeps the world alive. If all at once
Faith were to slacken,—that unconscious faith
Which must, I know, yet be the corner-stone
Of all believing,—birds now flying fearless
Across, would drop in terror to the earth;
Fishes would drown; and the all-governing reins
Would tangle in the frantic hands of God
And the worlds gallop headlong to destruction!

O God, I see it now, and my sick brain
Staggers and swoons! How often over me
Flashes this breathlessness of sudden sight
In which I see the universe unrolled
Before me like a scroll and read thereon
Chaos and Doom, where helpless planets whirl
Dizzily round and round and round and round,
Like tops across a table, gathering speed
With every spin, to waver on the edge
One instant—looking over—and the next
To shudder and lurch forward out of sight!

Ah, I am worn out—I am wearied out—
It is too much—I am but flesh and blood,
And I must sleep. Though you were dead again,
I am but flesh and blood and I must sleep.

THE SUICIDE[6]

"Curse thee, Life, I will live with thee no more!
Thou hast mocked me, starved me, beat my body sore!
And all for a pledge that was not pledged by me,
I have kissed thy crust and eaten sparingly
That I might eat again, and met thy sneers
With deprecations, and thy blows with tears,—
Aye, from thy glutted lash, glad, crawled away,
As if spent passion were a holiday!
And now I go. Nor threat, nor easy vow
Of tardy kindness can avail thee now
With me, whence fear and faith alike are flown;
Lonely I came, and I depart alone,
And know not where nor unto whom I go;
But that thou canst not follow me I know."

Thus I to Life, and ceased; but through my brain
My thought ran still, until I spake again:

"Ah, but I go not as I came,—no trace
Is mine to bear away of that old grace
I brought! I have been heated in thy fires,
Bent by thy hands, fashioned to thy desires,
Thy mark is on me! I am not the same
Nor ever more shall be, as when I came.
Ashes am I of all that once I seemed.
In me all's sunk that leapt, and all that dreamed
Is wakeful for alarm,—oh, shame to thee,
For the ill change that thou hast wrought in me

Who laugh no more nor lift my throat to sing!
Ah, Life, I would have been a pleasant thing
To have about the house when I was grown
If thou hadst left my little joys alone!
I asked of thee no favour save this one:
That thou wouldst leave me playing in the sun!
And this thou didst deny, calling my name
Insistently, until I rose and came.
I saw the sun no more.—It were not well
So long on these unpleasant thoughts to dwell,
Need I arise tomorrow and renew
Again my hated tasks, but I am through
With all things save my thoughts and this one night;
So that in truth I seem already quite
Free and remote from thee,—I feel no haste
And no reluctance to depart; I taste
Merely, with thoughtful mien, an unknown draught,
That in a little while I shall have quaffed."

Thus I to Life, and ceased, and slightly smiled,
Looking at nothing; and my thin dreams filed
Before me one by one till once again
I set new words unto an old refrain:

"Treasures thou hast that never have been mine!
Warm lights in many a secret chamber shine
Of thy gaunt house, and gusts of song have blown
Like blossoms out to me that sat alone!
And I have waited well for thee to show
If any share were mine,—and now I go!
Nothing I leave, and if I naught attain
I shall but come into mine own again!"

Thus I to Life, and ceased, and spake no more,
But turning, straightway sought a certain door
In the rear wall. Heavy it was, and low
And dark,—a way by which none e'er would go
That other exit had, and never knock
Was heard thereat,—bearing a curious lock,
Some chance had shown me fashioned faultily,
Whereof Life held content the useless key;
And great coarse hinges, thick and rough with rust,
Whose sudden voice across a silence must,
I knew, be harsh and horrible to hear,—
A strange door, ugly like a dwarf.—So near
I came I felt upon my feet the chill
Of acid wind creeping across the sill.
So stood longtime, till over me at last
Came weariness, and all things other passed
To make it room; the still night drifted deep
Like snow about me, and I longed for sleep.

But, suddenly, marking the morning hour,
Bayed the deep-throated bell within the tower!
Startled, I raised my head,—and with a shout
Laid hold upon the latch,—and was without.

Ah, long-forgotten, well-remembered road,
Leading me back unto my old abode,
My Father's house! There in the night I came,
And found them feasting, and all things the same
As they had been before. A splendour hung
Upon the walls, and such sweet songs were sung
As, echoing out of very long ago,

Had called me from the house of Life, I know.
So fair their raiment shone I looked in shame
On the unlovely garb in which I came;
Then straightway at my hesitancy mocked:
"It is my Father's house!" I said and knocked;
And the door opened. To the shining crowd
Tattered and dark I entered, like a cloud,
Seeing no face but His; to Him I crept,
And "Father!" I cried, and clasped His knees, and wept.[7]

Ah, days of joy that followed! All alone
I wandered through the house. My own, my own,
My own to touch, my own to taste and smell,
All I had lacked so long and loved so well!
None shook me out of sleep, nor hushed my song,
Nor called me in from the sunlight all day long.

I know not when the wonder came to me
Of what my Father's business might be,
And whither fared and on what errands bent
The tall and gracious messengers He sent.
Yet one day with no song from dawn till night
Wondering, I sat, and watched them out of sight.
And the next day I called; and on the third
Asked them if I might go,—but no one heard.
Then, sick with longing, I arose at last
And went unto my Father,—in that vast
Chamber wherein He for so many years
Has sat, surrounded by His charts and spheres.
"Father," I said, "Father, I cannot play
The harp that Thou didst give me, and all day

I sit in idleness, while to and fro
About me Thy serene, grave servants go;
And I am weary of my lonely ease.
Better a perilous journey overseas
Away from Thee, than this, the life I lead,
To sit all day in the sunshine like a weed
That grows to naught,—I love Thee more than they
Who serve Thee most; yet serve Thee in no way.
Father, I beg of Thee a little task
To dignify my days,—'tis all I ask
Forever, but forever, this denied,
I perish."
"Child," my Father's voice replied,
"All things thy fancy hath desired of me
Thou hast received. I have prepared for thee
Within my house a spacious chamber, where
Are delicate things to handle and to wear,
And all these things are thine. Dost thou love song?
My minstrels shall attend thee all day long.
Or sigh for flowers? My fairest gardens stand
Open as fields to thee on every hand.
And all thy days this word shall hold the same:
No pleasure shalt thou lack that thou shalt name.
But as for tasks—" He smiled, and shook His head;
"Thou hadst thy task, and laidst it by," He said.

GOD'S WORLD[8]

O world, I cannot hold thee close enough!
  Thy winds, thy wide grey skies!
  Thy mists, that roll and rise!
Thy woods, this autumn day, that ache and sag
And all but cry with colour! That gaunt crag
To crush! To lift the lean of that black bluff!
World, World, I cannot get thee close enough!

Long have I known a glory in it all,
    But never knew I this:
    Here such a passion is
As stretcheth me apart,—Lord, I do fear
Thou'st made the world too beautiful this year;
My soul is all but out of me,—let fall
No burning leaf; prithee, let no bird call.

AFTERNOON ON A HILL

I will be the gladdest thing
   Under the sun!
I will touch a hundred flowers
   And not pick one.

I will look at cliffs and clouds
   With quiet eyes,
Watch the wind bow down the grass,
   And the grass rise.

And when lights begin to show
   Up from the town,
I will mark which must be mine,
   And then start down!

SORROW

Sorrow like a ceaseless rain
    Beats upon my heart.
People twist and scream in pain,—
Dawn will find them still again;
This has neither wax nor wane,
    Neither stop nor start.

People dress and go to town;
    I sit in my chair.
All my thoughts are slow and brown:
Standing up or sitting down
Little matters, or what gown
    Or what shoes I wear.

TAVERN

I'll keep a little tavern
   Below the high hill's crest,
Wherein all grey-eyed people
   May sit them down and rest.

There shall be plates a-plenty,
   And mugs to melt the chill
Of all the grey-eyed people
   Who happen up the hill.

There sound will sleep the traveller,
   And dream his journey's end,
But I will rouse at midnight
   The falling fire to tend.

Aye, 'tis a curious fancy—
   But all the good I know
Was taught me out of two grey eyes
   A long time ago.

ASHES OF LIFE

Love has gone and left me and the days are all alike;
Eat I must, and sleep I will,—and would that night were here!
But ah!—to lie awake and hear the slow hours strike!
Would that it were day again!—with twilight near!

Love has gone and left me and I don't know what to do;
This or that or what you will is all the same to me;
But all the things that I begin I leave before I'm through,—
There's little use in anything as far as I can see.

Love has gone and left me,—and the neighbours knock and borrow,
And life goes on forever like the gnawing of a mouse,—
And tomorrow and tomorrow and tomorrow and tomorrow[9]
There's this little street and this little house.

THE LITTLE GHOST

I knew her for a little ghost
   That in my garden walked;
The wall is high—higher than most—
   And the green gate was locked.

And yet I did not think of that
   Till after she was gone—
I knew her by the broad white hat,
   All ruffled, she had on,

By the dear ruffles round her feet,
   By her small hands that hung
In their lace mitts, austere and sweet,
   Her gown's white folds among.

I watched to see if she would stay,
   What she would do—and oh!
She looked as if she liked the way
   I let my garden grow!

She bent above my favourite mint
   With conscious garden grace,
She smiled and smiled—there was no hint
   Of sadness in her face.

She held her gown on either side
   To let her slippers show,

And up the walk she went with pride,
The way great ladies go.

And where the wall is built in new,
And is of ivy bare,
She paused—then opened and passed through
A gate that once was there.

KIN TO SORROW

Am I kin to Sorrow,
That so oft
Falls the knocker of my door—
Neither loud nor soft,
But as long accustomed—
Under Sorrow's hand?
Marigolds around the step
And rosemary stand,
And then comes Sorrow—
And what does Sorrow care
For the rosemary
Or the marigolds there?
Am I kin to Sorrow?
Are we kin?
That so oft upon my door—
Oh, come in!

THREE SONGS OF SHATTERING

I

The first rose on my rose-tree
Budded, bloomed, and shattered,
During sad days when to me
Nothing mattered.

Grief of grief has drained me clean;
Still it seems a pity
No one saw,—it must have been
Very pretty.

II

Let the little birds sing;
Let the little lambs play;
Spring is here; and so 'tis spring;—
But not in the old way!

I recall a place
Where a plum-tree grew;
There you lifted up your face,
And blossoms covered you.

If the little birds sing,
And the little lambs play,
Spring is here; and so 'tis spring—
But not in the old way!

III

All the dog-wood blossoms are underneath the tree!
  Ere spring was going—ah, spring is gone!
And there comes no summer to the like of you and me,—
  Blossom time is early, but no fruit sets on.

All the dog-wood blossoms are underneath the tree,
  Browned at the edges, turned in a day;
And I would with all my heart they trimmed a mound for me,
  And weeds were tall on all the paths that led that way!

THE SHROUD

Death, I say, my heart is bowed
 Unto thine,—O mother!
This red gown will make a shroud
 Good as any other!

(I, that would not wait to wear
 My own bridal things,
In a dress dark as my hair
 Made my answerings.

I, to-night, that till he came
 Could not, could not wait,
In a gown as bright as flame
 Held for them the gate.)

Death, I say, my heart is bowed
 Unto thine,—O mother!
This red gown will make a shroud
 Good as any other!

THE DREAM

Love, if I weep it will not matter,
   And if you laugh I shall not care;
Foolish am I to think about it,
   But it is good to feel you there.

Love, in my sleep I dreamed of waking,—
   White and awful the moonlight reached
Over the floor, and somewhere, somewhere
   There was a shutter loose,—it screeched!—

Swung in the wind!—and no wind blowing!—
   I was afraid, and turned to you,
Put out my hand to you for comfort,—
   And you were gone! Cold, cold as dew,

Under my hand the moonlight lay!
   Love, if you laugh I shall not care,
But if I weep it will not matter,—
   Ah, it is good to feel you there!

INDIFFERENCE

I said,—for Love was laggard, oh, Love was slow
to come,—
"I'll hear his step and know his step when I am warm
in bed;
But I'll never leave my pillow, though there be some
As would let him in—and take him in with tears!"
I said.

I lay,—for Love was laggard, oh, he came not until
dawn,—
I lay and listened for his step and could not get
to sleep;
And he found me at my window with my big cloak on,
All sorry with the tears some folks might weep!

WITCH-WIFE[10]

She is neither pink nor pale,
And she never will be all mine;
She learned her hands in a fairy-tale,
And her mouth on a valentine.

She has more hair than she needs;
In the sun 'tis a woe to me!
And her voice is a string of coloured beads,
Or steps leading into the sea.

She loves me all that she can,
And her ways to my ways resign;
But she was not made for any man,
And she never will be all mine.

BLIGHT

Hard seeds of hate I planted
   That should by now be grown,—
Rough stalks, and from thick stamens
   A poisonous pollen blown,
And odours rank, unbreathable,
   From dark corollas thrown!

At dawn from my damp garden
   I shook the chilly dew;
The thin boughs locked behind me
   That sprang to let me through;
The blossoms slept,—I sought a place
   Where nothing lovely grew.

And there, when day was breaking,
   I knelt and looked around:
The light was near, the silence
   Was palpitant with sound;
I drew my hate from out my breast
   And thrust it in the ground.

Oh, ye so fiercely tended,
   Ye little seeds of hate!
I bent above your growing
   Early and noon and late,
Yet are ye drooped and pitiful,—
   I cannot rear ye straight!

The sun seeks out my garden,
No nook is left in shade,
No mist nor mold nor mildew
Endures on any blade,
Sweet rain slants under every bough:
Ye falter, and ye fade.

WHEN THE YEAR GROWS OLD

I cannot but remember
  When the year grows old—
October—November—
  How she disliked the cold![11]

She used to watch the swallows
  Go down across the sky,
And turn from the window
  With a little sharp sigh.

And often when the brown leaves
  Were brittle on the ground,
And the wind in the chimney
  Made a melancholy sound,

She had a look about her
  That I wish I could forget—
The look of a scared thing
  Sitting in a net!

Oh, beautiful at nightfall
  The soft spitting snow!
And beautiful the bare boughs
  Rubbing to and fro!

But the roaring of the fire,
  And the warmth of fur,

And the boiling of the kettle
   Were beautiful to her!

I cannot but remember
   When the year grows old—
October—November—
   How she disliked the cold!

Thou art not lovelier than lilacs,—no,
Nor honeysuckle; thou art not more fair
Than small white single poppies,—I can bear
Thy beauty; though I bend before thee, though
From left to right, not knowing where to go,
I turn my troubled eyes, nor here nor there
Find any refuge from thee, yet I swear
So has it been with mist,—with moonlight so.
Like him who day by day unto his draught
Of delicate poison adds him one drop more
Till he may drink unharmed the death of ten,
Even so, inured to beauty, who have quaffed
Each hour more deeply than the hour before,
I drink—and live—what has destroyed some men.

Time does not bring relief; you all have lied
Who told me time would ease me of my pain!
I miss him in the weeping of the rain;
I want him at the shrinking of the tide;
The old snows melt from every mountain-side,
And last year's leaves are smoke in every lane;
But last year's bitter loving must remain
Heaped on my heart, and my old thoughts abide.
There are a hundred places where I fear
To go,—so with his memory they brim.
And entering with relief some quiet place
Where never fell his foot or shone his face
I say, "There is no memory of him here!"
And so stand stricken, so remembering him.

Mindful of you the sodden earth in spring,
And all the flowers that in the springtime grow;
And dusty roads, and thistles, and the slow
Rising of the round moon; all throats that sing
The summer through, and each departing wing,
And all the nests that the bared branches show;
And all winds that in any weather blow,
And all the storms that the four seasons bring.
You go no more on your exultant feet
Up paths that only mist and morning knew;
Or watch the wind, or listen to the beat
Of a bird's wings too high in air to view,—
But you were something more than young and sweet
And fair,—and the long year remembers you.

Not in this chamber only at my birth—
When the long hours of that mysterious night
Were over, and the morning was in sight—
I cried, but in strange places, steppe and firth
I have not seen, through alien grief and mirth;
And never shall one room contain me quite
Who in so many rooms first saw the light,
Child of all mothers, native of the earth.
So is no warmth for me at any fire
Today, when the world's fire has burned so low;
I kneel, spending my breath in vain desire,
At that cold hearth which one time roared so strong:
And straighten back in weariness, and long
To gather up my little gods and go.

If I should learn, in some quite casual way,
That you were gone, not to return again—
Read from the back-page of a paper, say,
Held by a neighbor in a subway train,
How at the corner of this avenue
And such a street (so are the papers filled)
A hurrying man, who happened to be you,
At noon today had happened to be killed—
I should not cry aloud—I could not cry
Aloud, or wring my hands in such a place—
I should but watch the station lights rush by
With a more careful interest on my face;
Or raise my eyes and read with greater care
Where to store furs and how to treat the hair.

BLUEBEARD[12]

This door you might not open, and you did;
So enter now, and see for what slight thing
You are betrayed. . . . Here is no treasure hid,
No cauldron, no clear crystal mirroring
The sought-for Truth, no heads of women slain
For greed like yours, no writhings of distress;
But only what you see. . . . Look yet again:
An empty room, cobwebbed and comfortless.
Yet this alone out of my life I kept
Unto myself, lest any know me quite;
And you did so profane me when you crept
Unto the threshold of this room tonight
That I must never more behold your face.
This now is yours. I seek another place.

A FEW FIGS FROM THISTLES

FIRST FIG[1]

My candle burns at both ends;
  It will not last the night;
But ah, my foes, and oh, my friends—
  It gives a lovely light!

SECOND FIG

Safe upon the solid rock the ugly houses stand:
Come and see my shining palace built upon the sand!

RECUERDO[2]

We were very tired, we were very merry—
We had gone back and forth all night on the ferry.
It was bare and bright, and smelled like a stable—
But we looked into a fire, we leaned across a table,
We lay on a hill-top underneath the moon;
And the whistles kept blowing, and the dawn came soon.

We were very tired, we were very merry—
We had gone back and forth all night on the ferry;
And you ate an apple, and I ate a pear,
From a dozen of each we had bought somewhere;
And the sky went wan, and the wind came cold,
And the sun rose dripping, a bucketful of gold.

We were very tired, we were very merry,
We had gone back and forth all night on the ferry.
We hailed, "Good morrow, mother!" to a shawl-covered head,
And bought a morning paper, which neither of us read;
And she wept, "God bless you!" for the apples and pears,
And we gave her all our money but our subway fares.

THURSDAY

And if I loved you Wednesday,
  Well, what is that to you?
I do not love you Thursday—
  So much is true.

And why you come complaining
  Is more than I can see.
I loved you Wednesday,—yes—but what
  Is that to me?

TO THE NOT IMPOSSIBLE HIM

How shall I know, unless I go
To Cairo and Cathay,
Whether or not this blessèd spot
Is blest in every way?

Now it may be, the flower for me
Is this beneath my nose;
How shall I tell, unless I smell
The Carthaginian rose?

The fabric of my faithful love
No power shall dim or ravel
Whilst I stay here,—but oh, my dear,
If I should ever travel!

MACDOUGAL STREET[3]

As I went walking up and down to take the evening air,
(Sweet to meet upon the street, why must I be so shy?)
I saw him lay his hand upon her torn black hair;
("Little dirty Latin child, let the lady by!")

The women squatting on the stoops were slovenly and fat,
(Lay me out in organdie, lay me out in lawn!)
And everywhere I stepped there was a baby or a cat;
(Lord God in Heaven, will it never be dawn?)

The fruit-carts and clam-carts were ribald as a fair,
(Pink nets and wet shells trodden under heel)
She had haggled from the fruit-man of his rotting ware;
(I shall never get to sleep, the way I feel!)

He walked like a king through the filth and the clutter,
(Sweet to meet upon the street, why did you glance me by?)
But he caught the quaint Italian quip she flung him from the gutter;
(What can there be to cry about that I should lie and cry?)

He laid his darling hand upon her little black head,
(I wish I were a ragged child with ear-rings in my ears!)
And he said she was a baggage to have said what she had said;
(Truly I shall be ill unless I stop these tears!)

THE SINGING-WOMAN FROM THE WOOD'S EDGE[4]

What should I be but a prophet and a liar,
Whose mother was a leprechaun, whose father was a friar?
Teethed on a crucifix and cradled under water,
What should I be but the fiend's god-daughter?

And who should be my playmates but the adder and the frog,
That was got beneath a furze-bush and born in a bog?
And what should be my singing, that was christened at an altar,
But Aves and Credos and Psalms out of the Psalter?

You will see such webs on the wet grass, maybe,
As a pixie-mother weaves for her baby,
You will find such flame at the wave's weedy ebb
As flashes in the meshes of a mer-mother's web,

But there comes to birth no common spawn
From the love of a priest for a leprechaun,
And you never have seen and you never will see
Such things as the things that swaddled me!

After all's said and after all's done,
What should I be but a harlot and a nun?

In through the bushes, on any foggy day,
My Da would come a-swishing of the drops away,
With a prayer for my death and a groan for my birth,
A-mumbling of his beads for all that he was worth.

And there'd sit my Ma, with her knees beneath her chin,
A-looking in his face and a-drinking of it in,
And a-marking in the moss some funny little saying
That would mean just the opposite of all that he was
praying!

He taught me the holy-talk of Vesper and of Matin,
He heard me my Greek and he heard me my Latin,
He blessed me and crossed me to keep my soul from
evil,
And we watched him out of sight, and we conjured up
the devil!

Oh, the things I haven't seen and the things I haven't
known,
What with hedges and ditches till after I was grown,
And yanked both ways by my mother and my father,
With a "Which would you better?" and a "Which
would you rather?"

With him for a sire and her for a dam,
What should I be but just what I am?

SHE IS OVERHEARD SINGING

Oh, Prue she has a patient man,
  And Joan a gentle lover,
And Agatha's Arth' is a hug-the-hearth,—
  But my true love's a rover!

Mig, her man's as good as cheese
  And honest as a briar,
Sue tells her love what he's thinking of,—
  But my dear lad's a liar!

Oh, Sue and Prue and Agatha
  Are thick with Mig and Joan!
They bite their threads and shake their heads
  And gnaw my name like a bone;

And Prue says, "Mine's a patient man,
  As never snaps me up,"
And Agatha, "Arth' is a hug-the-hearth,
  Could live content in a cup;"

Sue's man's mind is like good jell—
  All one colour, and clear—
And Mig's no call to think at all
  What's to come next year,

While Joan makes boast of a gentle lad,
  That's troubled with that and this;—

But they all would give the life they live
  For a look from the man I kiss!

Cold he slants his eyes about,
  And few enough's his choice,—
Though he'd slip me clean for a nun, or a queen,
  Or a beggar with knots in her voice,—

And Agatha will turn awake
  While her good man sleeps sound,
And Mig and Sue and Joan and Prue
  Will hear the clock strike round,

For Prue she has a patient man,
  As asks not when or why,
And Mig and Sue have naught to do
  But peep who's passing by,

Joan is paired with a putterer
  That bastes and tastes and salts,
And Agatha's Arth' is a hug-the-hearth,—
  But my true love is false!

THE PRISONER

All right,
Go ahead!
What's in a name?
I guess I'll be locked into
As much as I'm locked out of!

THE UNEXPLORER

There was a road ran past our house
Too lovely to explore.
I asked my mother once—she said
That if you followed where it led
It brought you to the milk-man's door.
(That's why I have not travelled more.)

GROWN-UP

Was it for this I uttered prayers,
And sobbed and cursed and kicked the stairs,
That now, domestic as a plate,
I should retire at half-past eight?

THE PENITENT

I had a little Sorrow,
   Born of a little Sin,
I found a room all damp with gloom
   And shut us all within;
And, "Little Sorrow, weep," said I,
"And, Little Sin, pray God to die,
And I upon the floor will lie
   And think how bad I've been!"

Alas for pious planning—
   It mattered not a whit!
As far as gloom went in that room,
   The lamp might have been lit!
My little Sorrow would not weep,
My little Sin would go to sleep—
To save my soul I could not keep
   My graceless mind on it!

So up I got in anger,
   And took a book I had,
And put a ribbon on my hair
   To please a passing lad,
And, "One thing there's no getting by—
I've been a wicked girl," said I;
"But if I can't be sorry, why,
   I might as well be glad!"

DAPHNE[5]

Why do you follow me?—
Any moment I can be
Nothing but a laurel-tree.

Any moment of the chase
I can leave you in my place
A pink bough for your embrace.

Yet if over hill and hollow
Still it is your will to follow,
I am off;—to heel, Apollo![6]

PORTRAIT BY A NEIGHBOUR

Before she has her floor swept
  Or her dishes done,
Any day you'll find her
  A-sunning in the sun!

It's long after midnight
  Her key's in the lock,
And you never see her chimney smoke
  Till past ten o'clock!

She digs in her garden
  With a shovel and a spoon,
She weeds her lazy lettuce
  By the light of the moon,

She walks up the walk
  Like a woman in a dream,
She forgets she borrowed butter
  And pays you back cream!

Her lawn looks like a meadow,
  And if she mows the place
She leaves the clover standing
  And the Queen Anne's lace!

MIDNIGHT OIL

Cut if you will, with Sleep's dull knife,
  Each day to half its length, my friend,—
The years that Time takes off *my* life,
  He'll take from off the other end!

THE MERRY MAID

Oh, I am grown so free from care
 Since my heart broke!
I set my throat against the air,
 I laugh at simple folk!

There's little kind and little fair
 Is worth its weight in smoke
To me, that's grown so free from care
 Since my heart broke!

Lass, if to sleep you would repair
 As peaceful as you woke,
Best not besiege your lover there
 For just the words he spoke
To me, that's grown so free from care
 Since my heart broke!

TO KATHLEEN[7]

Still must the poet as of old,
In barren attic bleak and cold,
Starve, freeze, and fashion verses to
Such things as flowers and song and you;

Still as of old his being give
In Beauty's name, while she may live,
Beauty that may not die as long
As there are flowers and you and song.

TO S. M.[8]

(If He Should Lie A-dying)

I am not willing you should go
Into the earth, where Helen[9] went;
She is awake by now, I know.
Where Cleopatra's[10] anklets rust
You will not lie with my consent;
And Sappho[11] is a roving dust;
Cressid[12] could love again; Dido,[13]
Rotted in state, is restless still:
You leave me much against my will.

THE PHILOSOPHER

And what are you that, wanting you,
 I should be kept awake
As many nights as there are days
 With weeping for your sake?

And what are you that, missing you,
 As many days as crawl
I should be listening to the wind
 And looking at the wall?

I know a man that's a braver man
 And twenty men as kind,
And what are you, that you should be
 The one man in my mind?

Yet women's ways are witless ways,
 As any sage will tell,—
And what am I, that I should love
 So wisely and so well?[14]

I do but ask that you be always fair,
That I for ever may continue kind;
Knowing me what I am, you should not dare
To lapse from beauty ever, nor seek to bind
My alterable mood with lesser cords:
Weeping and such soft matters but invite
To further vagrancy, and bitter words
Chafe soon to irremediable flight.
Wherefore I pray you if you love me dearly
Less dear to hold me than your own bright charms,
Whence it may fall that until death or nearly
I shall not move to struggle from your arms;
Fade if you must; I would but bid you be
Like the sweet year, doing all things graciously.

Love, though for this you riddle me with darts,[15]
And drag me at your chariot till I die,—
Oh, heavy prince! Oh, panderer of hearts!—
Yet hear me tell how in their throats they lie
Who shout you mighty: thick about my hair,
Day in, day out, your ominous arrows purr,
Who still am free, unto no querulous care
A fool, and in no temple worshiper!
I, that have bared me to your quiver's fire,
Lifted my face into its puny rain,
Do wreathe you Impotent to Evoke Desire
As you are Powerless to Elicit Pain!
(Now will the god, for blasphemy so brave,
Punish me, surely, with the shaft I crave!)

I think I should have loved you presently,
And given in earnest words I flung in jest;
And lifted honest eyes for you to see,
And caught your hand against my cheek and breast;
And all my pretty follies flung aside
That won you to me, and beneath your gaze,
Naked of reticence and shorn of pride,
Spread like a chart my little wicked ways.
I, that had been to you, had you remained,
But one more waking from a recurrent dream,
Cherish no less the certain stakes I gained,
And walk your memory's halls, austere, supreme,
A ghost in marble of a girl you knew
Who would have loved you in a day or two.

Oh, think not I am faithful to a vow![16]
Faithless am I save to love's self alone.
Were you not lovely I would leave you now:
After the feet of beauty fly my own.
Were you not still my hunger's rarest food,
And water ever to my wildest thirst,
I would desert you—think not but I would!—
And seek another as I sought you first.
But you are mobile as the veering air,
And all your charms more changeful than the tide,
Wherefore to be inconstant is no care:
I have but to continue at your side.
So wanton, light and false, my love, are you,
I am most faithless when I most am true.

I shall forget you presently, my dear,
So make the most of this, your little day,
Your little month, your little half a year,
Ere I forget, or die, or move away,
And we are done forever; by and by
I shall forget you, as I said, but now,
If you entreat me with your loveliest lie
I will protest you with my favourite vow.[17]
I would indeed that love were longer-lived,
And oaths were not so brittle as they are,
But so it is, and nature has contrived
To struggle on without a break thus far,—
Whether or not we find what we are seeking
Is idle, biologically speaking.

SECOND APRIL[1]

SPRING[2]

To what purpose, April, do you return again?
Beauty is not enough.
You can no longer quiet me with the redness
Of little leaves opening stickily.
I know what I know.
The sun is hot on my neck as I observe
The spikes of the crocus.
The smell of the earth is good.
It is apparent that there is no death.
But what does that signify?
Not only under ground are the brains of men
Eaten by maggots.
Life in itself
Is nothing,
An empty cup, a flight of uncarpeted stairs.
It is not enough that yearly, down this hill,
April
Comes like an idiot, babbling and strewing flowers.

CITY TREES

The trees along this city street,
Save for the traffic and the trains,
Would make a sound as thin and sweet
As trees in country lanes.

And people standing in their shade
Out of a shower, undoubtedly
Would hear such music as is made
Upon a country tree.

Oh, little leaves that are so dumb
Against the shrieking city air,
I watch you when the wind has come,—
I know what sound is there.

THE BLUE-FLAG[3] IN THE BOG

God had called us, and we came;
  Our loved Earth to ashes left;
Heaven was a neighbour's house,
  Open flung to us, bereft.

Gay the lights of Heaven showed,
  And 'twas God who walked ahead;
Yet I wept along the road,
  Wanting my own house instead.

Wept unseen, unheeded cried,
  "All you things my eyes have kissed,
Fare you well! We meet no more,
  Lovely, lovely tattered mist!

Weary wings that rise and fall
  All day long above the fire!"
(Red with heat was every wall,
  Rough with heat was every wire)

"Fare you well, you little winds
  That the flying embers chase!
Fare you well, you shuddering day,
  With your hands before your face!

And, ah, blackened by strange blight,
  Or to a false sun unfurled,

Now forevermore goodbye,
All the gardens in the world!

On the windless hills of Heaven,
That I have no wish to see,
White, eternal lilies stand,
By a lake of ebony.

But the Earth forevermore
Is a place where nothing grows,—
Dawn will come, and no bud break;
Evening, and no blossom close.

Spring will come, and wander slow
Over an indifferent land,
Stand beside an empty creek,
Hold a dead seed in her hand."

God had called us, and we came,
But the blessèd road I trod
Was a bitter road to me,
And at heart I questioned God.

"Though in Heaven," I said, "be all
That the heart would most desire,
Held Earth naught save souls of sinners
Worth the saving from a fire?

Withered grass,—the wasted growing!
Aimless ache of laden boughs!"

Little things God had forgotten
 Called me, from my burning house.

"Though in Heaven," I said, "be all
 That the eye could ask to see,
All the things I ever knew
 Are this blaze in back of me."

"Though in Heaven," I said, "be all
 That the ear could think to lack,
All the things I ever knew
 Are this roaring at my back."

It was God who walked ahead,
 Like a shepherd to the fold;
In his footsteps fared the weak,
 And the weary and the old,

Glad enough of gladness over,
 Ready for the peace to be,—
But a thing God had forgotten
 Was the growing bones of me.

And I drew a bit apart,
 And I lagged a bit behind,
And I thought on Peace Eternal,
 Lest He look into my mind:

And I gazed upon the sky,
 And I thought of Heavenly Rest,—

And I slipped away like water
   Through the fingers of the blest!

All their eyes were fixed on Glory,
   Not a glance brushed over me;
"Alleluia! Alleluia!"
   Up the road,—and I was free.

And my heart rose like a freshet,
   And it swept me on before,
Giddy as a whirling stick,
   Till I felt the earth once more.

All the Earth was charred and black,
   Fire had swept from pole to pole;
And the bottom of the sea
   Was as brittle as a bowl;

And the timbered mountain-top
   Was as naked as a skull,—
Nothing left, nothing left,
   Of the Earth so beautiful!

"Earth," I said, "how can I leave you?"
   "You are all I have," I said;
"What is left to take my mind up,
   Living always, and you dead?"

"Speak!" I said, "Oh, tell me something!
   Make a sign that I can see!

For a keepsake! To keep always!
  Quick!—before God misses me!"

And I listened for a voice;—
  But my heart was all I heard;
Not a screech-owl, not a loon,
  Not a tree-toad said a word.

And I waited for a sign;—
  Coals and cinders, nothing more;
And a little cloud of smoke
  Floating on a valley floor.

And I peered into the smoke
  Till it rotted, like a fog:—
There, encompassed round by fire,
  Stood a blue-flag in a bog!

Little flames came wading out,
  Straining, straining towards its stem,
But it was so blue and tall
  That it scorned to think of them!

Red and thirsty were their tongues,
  As the tongues of wolves must be,
But it was so blue and tall—
  Oh, I laughed, I cried, to see!

All my heart became a tear,
  All my soul became a tower,
Never loved I anything
  As I loved that tall blue flower!

It was all the little boats
That had ever sailed the sea,
It was all the little books
That had gone to school with me;

On its roots like iron claws
Rearing up so blue and tall,—
It was all the gallant Earth
With its back against a wall!

In a breath, ere I had breathed,—
Oh, I laughed, I cried, to see!—
I was kneeling at its side,
And it leaned its head on me!

Crumbling stones and sliding sand
Is the road to Heaven now;
Icy at my straining knees
Drags the awful under-tow;

Soon but stepping-stones of dust
Will the road to Heaven be,—
Father, Son and Holy Ghost,
Reach a hand and rescue me!

"There—there, my blue-flag flower;
Hush—hush—go to sleep;
That is only God you hear,
Counting up His folded sheep!

Lullabye—lullabye—
   That is only God that calls,
Missing me, seeking me,
   Ere the road to nothing falls!

He will set His mighty feet
   Firmly on the sliding sand;
Like a little frightened bird
   I will creep into His hand;

I will tell Him all my grief,
   I will tell Him all my sin;
He will give me half His robe
   For a cloak to wrap you in.

Lullabye—lullabye—"
   Rocks the burnt-out planet free!—
Father, Son and Holy Ghost,
   Reach a hand and rescue me![4]

Ah, the voice of love at last!
   Lo, at last the face of light!
And the whole of His white robe
   For a cloak against the night!

And upon my heart asleep
   All the things I ever knew!—
"Holds Heaven not some cranny, Lord,
   For a flower so tall and blue?"

All's well and all's well![5]
Gay the lights of Heaven show!
In some moist and Heavenly place
We will set it out to grow.

JOURNEY[6]

Ah, could I lay me down in this long grass
And close my eyes, and let the quiet wind
Blow over me—I am so tired, so tired
Of passing pleasant places! All my life,
Following Care along the dusty road,
Have I looked back at loveliness and sighed;
Yet at my hand an unrelenting hand
Tugged ever, and I passed. All my life long
Over my shoulder have I looked at peace;
And now I fain would lie in this long grass
And close my eyes.

Yet onward!

Cat-birds call
Through the long afternoon, and creeks at dusk
Are guttural. Whip-poor-wills wake and cry,
Drawing the twilight close about their throats.
Only my heart makes answer. Eager vines
Go up the rocks and wait; flushed apple-trees
Pause in their dance and break the ring for me;
Dim, shady wood-roads, redolent of fern
And bayberry, that through sweet bevies thread
Of round-faced roses, pink and petulant,
Look back and beckon ere they disappear.
Only my heart, only my heart responds.

Yet, ah, my path is sweet on either side
All through the dragging day,—sharp underfoot

And hot, and like dead mist the dry dust hangs—
But far, oh, far as passionate eye can reach,
And long, ah, long as rapturous eye can cling,
The world is mine: blue hill, still silver lake,
Broad field, bright flower, and the long white road;
A gateless garden, and an open path;
My feet to follow, and my heart to hold.

EEL-GRASS

No matter what I say,
  All that I really love
Is the rain that flattens on the bay,
  And the eel-grass in the cove;
The jingle-shells that lie and bleach
  At the tide-line, and the trace
Of higher tides along the beach:
  Nothing in this place.

ELEGY BEFORE DEATH

There will be rose and rhododendron
  When you are dead and under ground;
Still will be heard from white syringas
  Heavy with bees, a sunny sound;

Still will the tamaracks be raining
  After the rain has ceased, and still
Will there be robins in the stubble,
  Grey sheep upon the warm green hill.

Spring will not ail nor autumn falter;
  Nothing will know that you are gone,—
Saving alone some sullen plough-land
  None but yourself sets foot upon;

Saving the may-weed and the pig-weed
  Nothing will know that you are dead,—
These, and perhaps a useless wagon
  Standing beside some tumbled shed.

Oh, there will pass with your great passing
  Little of beauty not your own,—
Only the light from common water,
  Only the grace from simple stone!

THE BEAN-STALK[7]

Ho, Giant! This is I!
I have built me a bean-stalk into your sky!
La,—but it's lovely, up so high!

This is how I came,—I put
Here my knee, there my foot,
Up and up, from shoot to shoot—
And the blessèd bean-stalk thinning
Like the mischief all the time,
Till it took me rocking, spinning,
In a dizzy, sunny circle,
Making angles with the root,
Far and out above the cackle
Of the city I was born in,
Till the little dirty city
In the light so sheer and sunny
Shone as dazzling bright and pretty
As the money that you find
In a dream of finding money—
What a wind! What a morning!—
Till the tiny, shiny city,
When I shot a glance below,
Shaken with a giddy laughter,
Sick and blissfully afraid,
Was a dew-drop on a blade,
And a pair of moments after
Was the whirling guess I made,—
And the wind was like a whip

Cracking past my icy ears,
And my hair stood out behind,
And my eyes were full of tears,
Wide-open and cold,
More tears than they could hold,
The wind was blowing so,
And my teeth were in a row,
Dry and grinning,
And I felt my foot slip,
And I scratched the wind and whined,
And I clutched the stalk and jabbered,
With my eyes shut blind,—
What a wind! What a wind!

Your broad sky, Giant,
Is the shelf of a cupboard;
I make bean-stalks, I'm
A builder, like yourself,
But bean-stalks is my trade,
I couldn't make a shelf,
Don't know how they're made,
Now, a bean-stalk is more pliant—
La, what a climb!

WEEDS

White with daisies and red with sorrel
   And empty, empty under the sky!—
Life is a quest and love a quarrel—
   Here is a place for me to lie.

Daisies spring from damnèd seeds,
   And this red fire that here I see
Is a worthless crop of crimson weeds,
   Cursed by farmers thriftily.

But here, unhated for an hour,
   The sorrel runs in ragged flame,
The daisy stands, a bastard flower,
   Like flowers that bear an honest name.

And here a while, where no wind brings
   The baying of a pack athirst,
May sleep the sleep of blessèd things,
   The blood too bright, the brow accurst.

PASSER MORTUUS EST[8]

Death devours all lovely things:
  Lesbia with her sparrow[9]
Shares the darkness,—presently
  Every bed is narrow.

Unremembered as old rain
  Dries the sheer libation;
And the little petulant hand
  Is an annotation.

After all, my erstwhile dear,
  My no longer cherished,
Need we say it was not love,
  Just because it perished?

PASTORAL

If it were only still!—
With far away the shrill
Crying of a cock;
Or the shaken bell
From a cow's throat
Moving through the bushes;
Or the soft shock
Of wizened apples falling
From an old tree
In a forgotten orchard
Upon the hilly rock!

Oh, grey hill,
Where the grazing herd
Licks the purple blossom,
Crops the spiky weed!
Oh, stony pasture,
Where the tall mullein
Stands up so sturdy
On its little seed!

ASSAULT

I had forgotten how the frogs must sound
After a year of silence, else I think
I should not so have ventured forth alone
At dusk upon this unfrequented road.

I am waylaid by Beauty. Who will walk
Between me and the crying of the frogs?
Oh, savage Beauty, suffer me to pass,
That am a timid woman, on her way
From one house to another!

TRAVEL

The railroad track is miles away,
And the day is loud with voices speaking,
Yet there isn't a train goes by all day
But I hear its whistle shrieking.

All night there isn't a train goes by,
Though the night is still for sleep and dreaming,
But I see its cinders red on the sky,
And hear its engine steaming.

My heart is warm with the friends I make,
And better friends I'll not be knowing;
Yet there isn't a train I wouldn't take,
No matter where it's going.

LOW-TIDE

These wet rocks where the tide has been,
  Barnacled white and weeded brown
And slimed beneath to a beautiful green,
  These wet rocks where the tide went down
Will show again when the tide is high
  Faint and perilous, far from shore,
No place to dream, but a place to die:
  The bottom of the sea once more.

There was a child that wandered through
  A giant's empty house all day,—
House full of wonderful things and new,
  But no fit place for a child to play!

SONG OF A SECOND APRIL[10]

April this year, not otherwise
   Than April of a year ago,
Is full of whispers, full of sighs,
   Of dazzling mud and dingy snow;
   Hepaticas that pleased you so
Are here again, and butterflies.

There rings a hammering all day,
   And shingles lie about the doors;
In orchards near and far away
   The grey wood-pecker taps and bores;
   And men are merry at their chores,
And children earnest at their play.

The larger streams run still and deep,
   Noisy and swift the small brooks run;
Among the mullein stalks the sheep
   Go up the hillside in the sun,
   Pensively,—only you are gone,
You that alone I cared to keep.

ROSEMARY

For the sake of some things
That be now no more
I will strew rushes
On my chamber-floor,
I will plant bergamot
At my kitchen-door.

For the sake of dim things
That were once so plain
I will set a barrel
Out to catch the rain,
I will hang an iron pot
On an iron crane.

Many things be dead and gone
That were brave and gay;
For the sake of these things
I will learn to say,
"An it please you, gentle sirs,"
"Alack!" and "Well-a-day!"

THE POET AND HIS BOOK[11]

Down, you mongrel, Death!
Back into your kennel!
I have stolen breath
In a stalk of fennel!
You shall scratch and you shall whine
Many a night, and you shall worry
Many a bone, before you bury
One sweet bone of mine!

When shall I be dead?
When my flesh is withered,
And above my head
Yellow pollen gathered
All the empty afternoon?
When sweet lovers pause and wonder
Who am I that lie thereunder,
Hidden from the moon?

This my personal death?—
That my lungs be failing
To inhale the breath
Others are exhaling?
This my subtle spirit's end?—
Ah, when the thawed winter splashes
Over these chance dust and ashes,
Weep not me, my friend!

Me, by no means dead
  In that hour, but surely
When this book, unread,
  Rots to earth obscurely,
And no more to any breast,
  Close against the clamorous swelling
  Of the thing there is no telling,
Are these pages pressed!

When this book is mould,
  And a book of many
Waiting to be sold
  For a casual penny,
In a little open case,
  In a street unclean and cluttered,
  Where a heavy mud is spattered
From the passing drays,

Stranger, pause and look;
  From the dust of ages
Lift this little book,
  Turn the tattered pages,
Read me, do not let me die!
  Search the fading letters, finding
  Steadfast in the broken binding
All that once was I!

When these veins are weeds,
  When these hollowed sockets
Watch the rooty seeds
  Bursting down like rockets,

And surmise the spring again,
  Or, remote in that black cupboard,
  Watch the pink worms writhing upward
At the smell of rain,

Boys and girls that lie
  Whispering in the hedges,
Do not let me die,
  Mix me with your pledges;
Boys and girls that slowly walk
  In the woods, and weep, and quarrel,
  Staring past the pink wild laurel,
Mix me with your talk,

Do not let me die!
  Farmers at your raking,
When the sun is high,
  While the hay is making,
When, along the stubble strewn,
  Withering on their stalks uneaten,
  Strawberries turn dark and sweeten
In the lapse of noon;

Shepherds on the hills,
  In the pastures, drowsing
To the tinkling bells
  Of the brown sheep browsing;
Sailors crying through the storm;
  Scholars at your study; hunters
  Lost amid the whirling winter's
Whiteness uniform;

Men that long for sleep;
   Men that wake and revel;—
If an old song leap
   To your senses' level
At such moments, may it be
   Sometimes, though a moment only,
   Some forgotten, quaint and homely
Vehicle of me!

Women at your toil,
   Women at your leisure
Till the kettle boil,
   Snatch of me your pleasure,
Where the broom-straw marks the leaf;
   Women quiet with your weeping
   Lest you wake a workman sleeping,
Mix me with your grief!

Boys and girls that steal
   From the shocking laughter
Of the old, to kneel
   By a dripping rafter
Under the discoloured eaves,
   Out of trunks with hingeless covers
   Lifting tales of saints and lovers,
Travellers, goblins, thieves,

Suns that shine by night,
   Mountains made from valleys,—
Bear me to the light,
   Flat upon your bellies
By the webby window lie,
   Where the little flies are crawling,

Read me, margin me with scrawling,
Do not let me die!

Sexton,[12] *ply your trade!*
In a shower of gravel
Stamp upon your spade!
Many a rose shall ravel,
Many a metal wreath shall rust
In the rain, and I go singing
Through the lots where you are flinging
Yellow clay on dust!

ALMS

My heart is what it was before,
   A house where people come and go;
But it is winter with your love,
   The sashes are beset with snow.

I light the lamp and lay the cloth,
   I blow the coals to blaze again;
But it is winter with your love,
   The frost is thick upon the pane.

I know a winter when it comes:
   The leaves are listless on the boughs;
I watched your love a little while,
   And brought my plants into the house.

I water them and turn them south,
   I snap the dead brown from the stem;
But it is winter with your love,
   I only tend and water them.

There was a time I stood and watched
   The small, ill-natured sparrows' fray;
I loved the beggar that I fed,
   I cared for what he had to say,

I stood and watched him out of sight;
   Today I reach around the door

And set a bowl upon the step;
My heart is what it was before,

But it is winter with your love;
I scatter crumbs upon the sill,
And close the window,—and the birds
May take or leave them, as they will.

INLAND

People that build their houses inland,
  People that buy a plot of ground
Shaped like a house, and build a house there,
  Far from the sea-board, far from the sound

Of water sucking the hollow ledges,
  Tons of water striking the shore,—
What do they long for, as I long for
  One salt smell of the sea once more?

People the waves have not awakened,
  Spanking the boats at the harbour's head,
What do they long for, as I long for,—
  Starting up in my inland bed,

Beating the narrow walls, and finding
  Neither a window nor a door,
Screaming to God for death by drowning,—
  One salt taste of the sea once more?

TO A POET THAT DIED YOUNG[13]

Minstrel, what have you to do
With this man that, after you,
Sharing not your happy fate,
Sat as England's Laureate?[14]
Vainly, in these iron days,
Strives the poet in your praise,
Minstrel, by whose singing side
Beauty walked, until you died.

Still, though none should hark again,
Drones the blue-fly in the pane,
Thickly crusts the blackest moss,[15]
Blows the rose its musk across,
Floats the boat that is forgot
None the less to Camelot.[16]

Many a bard's untimely death
Lends unto his verses breath;
Here's a song was never sung:
Growing old is dying young.[17]
Minstrel, what is this to you:
That a man you never knew,
When your grave was far and green,
Sat and gossipped with a queen?

Thalia[18] knows how rare a thing
Is it, to grow old and sing,

When the brown and tepid tide
Closes in on every side.
Who shall say if Shelley's gold[19]
Had withstood it to grow old?

WRAITH

"Thin Rain, whom are you haunting,
  That you haunt my door?"
Surely it is not I she's wanting . . .
  Someone living here before!
"Nobody's in the house but me:
You may come in if you like and see."

Thin as thread, with exquisite fingers,—
  Ever seen her, any of you?—
Grey shawl, and leaning on the wind,
  And the garden showing through?

Glimmering eyes,—and silent, mostly,
  Sort of a whisper, sort of a purr,
Asking something, asking it over,
  If you get a sound from her.—

Ever see her, any of you?—
  Strangest thing I've ever known,—
Every night since I moved in,
  And I came to be alone.

"Thin Rain, hush with your knocking!
  You may not come in!
This is I that you hear rocking;
  Nobody's with me, nor has been!"

Curious, how she tried the window,—
  Odd, the way she tries the door,—
Wonder just what sort of people
  Could have had this house before . . .

EBB

I know what my heart is like
   Since your love died:
It is like a hollow ledge
Holding a little pool
   Left there by the tide,
   A little tepid pool,
Drying inward from the edge.

ELAINE[20]

Oh, come again to Astolat!
I will not ask you to be kind.
And you may go when you will go,
And I will stay behind.

I will not say how dear you are,
Or ask you if you hold me dear,
Or trouble you with things for you,
The way I did last year.

So still the orchard, Lancelot,
So very still the lake shall be,
You could not guess—though you should guess—
What is become of me.

So wide shall be the garden-walk,
The garden-seat so very wide,
You needs must think—if you should think—
The lily maid had died.

Save that, a little way away,
I'd watch you for a little while,
To see you speak, the way you speak,
And smile,—if you should smile.

BURIAL

Mine is a body that should die at sea!
 And have for a grave, instead of a grave
Six feet deep and the length of me,
 All the water that is under the wave!

And terrible fishes to seize my flesh,
 Such as a living man might fear,
And eat me while I am firm and fresh,—
 Not wait till I've been dead for a year!

MARIPOSA[21]

Butterflies are white and blue
In this field we wander through.
Suffer me to take your hand.
Death comes in a day or two.

All the things we ever knew
Will be ashes in that hour:
Mark the transient butterfly,
How he hangs upon the flower.

Suffer me to take your hand.
Suffer me to cherish you
Till the dawn is in the sky.
Whether I be false or true,
Death comes in a day or two.

THE LITTLE HILL[22]

Oh, here the air is sweet and still,
And soft's the grass to lie on;
And far away's the little hill
They took for Christ to die on.

And there's a hill across the brook,
And down the brook's another;
But, oh, the little hill they took,—
I think I am its mother!

The moon that saw Gethsemane,
I watch it rise and set;
It has so many things to see,
They help it to forget.

But little hills that sit at home
So many hundred years,
Remember Greece, remember Rome,
Remember Mary's tears.

And far away in Palestine,
Sadder than any other,
Grieves still the hill that I call mine,—
I think I am its mother.

DOUBT NO MORE THAT OBERON

Doubt no more that Oberon[23]—
Never doubt that Pan[24]
Lived, and played a reed, and ran
After nymphs in a dark forest,
In the merry, credulous days,—
Lived, and led a fairy band
Over the indulgent land!

Ah, for in this dourest, sorest
Age man's eye has looked upon,
Death to fauns and death to fays,[25]
Still the dog-wood dares to raise—
Healthy tree, with trunk and root—
Ivory bowls that bear no fruit,
And the starlings and the jays—
Birds that cannot even sing—
Dare to come again in spring!

LAMENT[26]

Listen, children:
Your father is dead.
From his old coats
I'll make you little jackets;
I'll make you little trousers
From his old pants.
There'll be in his pockets
Things he used to put there,
Keys and pennies
Covered with tobacco;
Dan shall have the pennies
To save in his bank;
Anne shall have the keys
To make a pretty noise with.
Life must go on,
And the dead be forgotten;
Life must go on,
Though good men die;

Anne, eat your breakfast;
Dan, take your medicine;
Life must go on;
I forget just why.

EXILED

Searching my heart for its true sorrow,
This is the thing I find to be:
That I am weary of words and people,
Sick of the city, wanting the sea;

Wanting the sticky, salty sweetness
Of the strong wind and shattered spray;
Wanting the loud sound and the soft sound
Of the big surf that breaks all day.

Always before about my dooryard,
Marking the reach of the winter sea,
Rooted in sand and dragging drift-wood,
Straggled the purple wild sweet-pea;

Always I climbed the wave at morning,
Shook the sand from my shoes at night,
That now am caught beneath great buildings,
Stricken with noise, confused with light.

If I could hear the green piles groaning
Under the windy wooden piers,
See once again the bobbing barrels,
And the black sticks that fence the weirs,

If I could see the weedy mussels
Crusting the wrecked and rotting hulls,

Hear once again the hungry crying
   Overhead, of the wheeling gulls,

Feel once again the shanty straining
   Under the turning of the tide,
Fear once again the rising freshet,
   Dread the bell in the fog outside,

I should be happy!—that was happy
   All day long on the coast of Maine;
I have a need to hold and handle
   Shells and anchors and ships again!

I should be happy . . . that am happy
   Never at all since I came here.
I am too long away from water.
   I have a need of water near.

THE DEATH OF AUTUMN[27]

When reeds are dead and a straw to thatch the marshes,
And feathered pampas-grass rides into the wind
Like agèd warriors westward, tragic, thinned
Of half their tribe; and over the flattened rushes,
Stripped of its secret, open, stark and bleak,
Blackens afar the half-forgotten creek,—
Then leans on me the weight of the year, and crushes
My heart. I know that Beauty must ail and die,
And will be born again,—but ah, to see
Beauty stiffened, staring up at the sky!
Oh, Autumn! Autumn!—What is the Spring to me?

ODE TO SILENCE[28]

Aye, but she?
Your other sister and my other soul,
Grave Silence, lovelier
Than the three loveliest maidens, what of her?
Clio,[29] not you,
Not you, Calliope,[30]
Nor all your wanton line,
Not Great Apollo's[31] self shall comfort me
For Silence once departed,
For her the cool-tongued, her the tranquil-hearted,
Whom evermore I follow wistfully,
Wandering Heaven and Earth and Hell and the four
seasons through;
Thalia,[32] not you,
Not you, Melpomene,[33]
Not your incomparable feet, O thin Terpsichore,[34]
I seek in this great hall,
But one more pale, more pensive, most beloved
of you all.

I seek her from afar.
I come from temples where her altars are;
From groves that bear her name;—
Noisy with stricken victims now and sacrificial flame,
And cymbals struck on high and strident faces
Obstreperous in her praise
They neither love nor know,

A goddess of gone days,
Departed long ago,
Abandoning the invaded shrines and fanes
Of her old sanctuary,
A deity obscure and legendary,
Of whom there now remains,
For sages to decipher and priests to garble,
Only and for a little while her letters wedged in marble;
Which even now, behold, the friendly mumbling rain
erases,
And the inarticulate snow,
Leaving at last of her least signs and traces
None whatsoever, nor whither she is vanished from these
places.

"She will love well," I said,
"If love be of that heart inhabiter,
The flowers of the dead:
The red anemone that with no sound
Moves in the wind; and from another wound
That sprang, the heavily-sweet blue hyacinth,
That blossoms underground;
And sallow poppies, will be dear to her.
And will not Silence know
In the black shade of what obsidian steep
Stiffens the white narcissus numb with sleep?
(Seed which Demeter's daughter[35] bore from home,
Uptorn by desperate fingers long ago,
Reluctant even as she,
Undone Persephone,[36]
And even as she, set out again to grow,
In twilight, in perdition's lean and inauspicious loam)

She will love well," I said,
"The flowers of the dead.
Where dark Persephone the winter round,
Uncomforted for home, uncomforted,
Lacking a sunny southern slope in northern Sicily,
With sullen pupils focussed on a dream
Stares on the stagnant stream
That moats the unequivocable battlements of Hell,
There, there will she be found,
She that is Beauty veiled from men and Music
in a swound."
"I long for Silence as they long for breath
Whose helpless nostrils drink the bitter sea;
What thing can be
So stout, what so redoubtable, in Death
What fury, what considerable rage, if only she,
Upon whose icy breast,
Unquestioned, uncaressed,
One time I lay,
And whom always I lack,
Even to this day,
Being by no means from that frigid bosom weaned away,
If only she therewith be given me back?"

I sought her down that dolourous labyrinth,
Wherein no shaft of sunlight ever fell,
And in among the bloodless everywhere
I sought her; but the air,
Breathed many times and spent,
Was fretful with a whispering discontent;
And questioning me, importuning me to tell
Some slightest tidings of the light of day they know
no more,

Plucking my sleeve, the eager shades were with me
where I went.
I paused at every grievous door,
And harked a moment, holding up my hand,—and for a
space
A hush was on them, while they watched my face;
And then they fell a-whispering as before;
So that I smiled at them and left them, seeing she was
not there.

I sought her, too,
Among the upper gods, although I knew
She was not like to be where feasting is,
Nor near to Heaven's lord,
Being a thing abhorred
And shunned of him, although a child of his,
(Not yours, not yours: to you she owes not breath,
Mother of Song, being sown of Zeus[37] upon a dream
of Death).

Fearing to pass unvisited some place
And later learn, too late, how all the while,
With her still face,
She had been standing there and seen me pass, without
a smile,
I sought her even to the sagging board whereat
The stout immortals sat;
But such a laughter shook the mighty hall
No one could hear me say:
Had she been seen upon the Hill[38] that day?
And no one knew at all
How long I stood, or when at last I sighed and
went away.

There is a garden lying in a lull
Between the mountains and the mountainous sea . . .
I know not where; but which a dream diurnal
Paints on my lids a moment, till the hull
Be lifted from the kernel,
And Slumber fed to me.
Your foot-print is not there, Mnemosene,[39]
Though it would seem a ruined place and after
Your lichenous heart, being full
Of broken columns, caryatides[40]
Thrown to the earth and fallen forward on their jointless
knees;
And urns funereal altered into dust
Minuter than the ashes of the dead;
And Psyche's lamp[41] out of the earth up-thrust,
Dripping itself in marble oil on what was once the bed
Of Love, and his young body asleep, but now is dust
instead.
There twists the bitter-sweet, the white wisteria
Fastens its fingers in the strangling wall,
And the wide crannies quicken with bright weeds;
There dumbly like a worm all day the still white orchid
feeds;
But never an echo of your daughters' laughter
Is there, nor any sign of you at all
Swells fungous from the rotten bough, grey mother
of Pieria![42]

Only her shadow once upon a stone
I saw,—and, lo, the shadow and the garden, too,
were gone.

I tell you, you have done her body an ill,
You chatterers, you noisy crew!
She is not anywhere!
I sought her in deep Hell;
And through the world as well;
I thought of Heaven and I sought her there:
Above nor under ground
Is Silence to be found,
That was the very warp and woof of you,
Lovely before your songs began and after they were
    through!
Oh, say if on this hill
Somewhere your sister's body lies in death,
So I may follow there, and make a wreath
Of my locked hands, that on her quiet breast
Shall lie till age has withered them!

(Ah, sweetly from the rest
I see
Turn and consider me
Compassionate Euterpe!)[43]

"There is a gate beyond the gate of Death,
Beyond the gate of everlasting Life,
Beyond the gates of Heaven and Hell," she saith,
"Whereon but to believe is horror!
Whereon to meditate engendereth
Even in deathless spirits such as I
A tumult in the breath,
A chilling of the inexhaustible blood
Even in my veins that never will be dry,
And in the austere, divine monotony

That is my being, the madness of an unaccustomed
mood.
This is her province whom you lack and seek:
And seek her not elsewhere.
Hell is a thoroughfare
For pilgrims,—Herakles,[44]
And he that loved Euridice too well,[45]
Have walked therein; and many more than these;
And witnessed the desire and the despair
Of souls that passed reluctantly and sicken for the air;
You, too, have entered Hell,
And issued thence; but thence whereof I speak
None has returned;—for thither fury brings
Only the driven ghosts of them that flee before all things.
Oblivion is the name of this abode: and she is there."

O radiant Song! O gracious Memory!
Be long upon this height
I shall not climb again!
I know the way you mean,—the little night,
And the long empty day,—never to see
Again the angry light,
Or hear the hungry noises cry my brain!

Ah, but she,
Your other sister and my other soul,
She shall again be mine.
And I shall drink her from a silver bowl,
A chilly thin green wine,
Not bitter to the taste,
Not sweet,
Not of your press, O restless, clamourous Nine,—

To foam beneath the frantic hoofs of mirth—
But savouring faintly of the acid earth
And trod by pensive feet
From perfect clusters ripened without haste
Out of the urgent heat
In some clear glimmering vaulted twilight
under the odourous vine.

Lift up your lyres! Sing on!
But as for me, I seek your sister whither she is gone.

MEMORIAL TO D. C.[46]

(Vassar College, 1918)

O, loveliest throat of all sweet throats,
Where now no more the music is,
With hands that wrote you little notes
I write you little elegies!

I
Epitaph

Heap not on this mound
Roses that she loved so well;
Why bewilder her with roses,
That she cannot see or smell?

She is happy where she lies
With the dust upon her eyes.

II

Prayer to Persephone[47]

Be to her, Persephone,
All the things I might not be;
Take her head upon your knee.
She that was so proud and wild,
Flippant, arrogant and free,
She that had no need of me,
Is a little lonely child
Lost in Hell,—Persephone,
Take her head upon your knee;
Say to her, "My dear, my dear,
It is not so dreadful here."

III

Chorus

Give away her gowns,
Give away her shoes;
She has no more use
For her fragrant gowns;
Take them all down,
Blue, green, blue,
Lilac, pink, blue,
From their padded hangers;
She will dance no more
In her narrow shoes;
Sweep her narrow shoes
From the closet floor.

IV
Dirge

Boys and girls that held her dear,
  Do your weeping now;
All you loved of her lies here.

Brought to earth the arrogant brow,
  And the withering tongue
Chastened; do your weeping now.

Sing whatever songs are sung,
  Wind whatever wreath,
For a playmate perished young,
  For a spirit spent in death.

Boys and girls that held her dear,
All you loved of her lies here.

V
Elegy

Let them bury your big eyes
In the secret earth securely,
Your thin fingers, and your fair,
Soft, indefinite-coloured hair,—
All of these in some way, surely,
From the secret earth shall rise;
Not for these I sit and stare,
Broken and bereft completely:
Your young flesh that sat so neatly
On your little bones will sweetly
Blossom in the air.

But your voice . . . never the rushing
Of a river underground,
Not the rising of the wind
In the trees before the rain,
Not the woodcock's watery call,
Not the note the white-throat utters,
Not the feet of children pushing
Yellow leaves along the gutters
In the blue and bitter fall,
Shall content my musing mind
For the beauty of that sound
That in no new way at all
Ever will be heard again.

Sweetly through the sappy stalk
Of the vigourous weed,

Holding all it held before,
Cherished by the faithful sun,
On and on eternally
Shall your altered fluid run,
Bud and bloom and go to seed:
But your singing days are done;
But the music of your talk
Never shall the chemistry
Of the secret earth restore.
All your lovely words are spoken.
Once the ivory box is broken,
Beats the golden bird no more.

WILD SWANS[48]

I looked in my heart while the wild swans went over.
And what did I see I had not seen before?
Only a question less or a question more;
Nothing to match the flight of wild birds flying.
Tiresome heart, forever living and dying,
House without air, I leave you and lock your door.
Wild swans, come over the town, come over
The town again, trailing your legs and crying!

We talk of taxes, and I call you friend;
Well, such you are,—but well enough we know
How thick about us root, how rankly grow
Those subtle weeds no man has need to tend,
That flourish through neglect, and soon must send
Perfume too sweet upon us and overthrow
Our steady senses; how such matters go
We are aware, and how such matters end.
Yet shall be told no meagre passion here;
With lovers such as we forevermore
Isolde[49] drinks the draught, and Guinevere[50]
Receives the Table's ruin[51] through her door,
Francesca,[52] with the loud surf at her ear,[53]
Lets fall the coloured book upon the floor.

Into the golden vessel of great song[54]
Let us pour all our passion; breast to breast
Let other lovers lie, in love and rest;
Not we,—articulate, so, but with the tongue
Of all the world: the churning blood, the long
Shuddering quiet, the desperate hot palms pressed
Sharply together upon the escaping guest,
The common soul, unguarded, and grown strong.
Longing alone is singer to the lute;
Let still on nettles in the open sigh
The minstrel, that in slumber is as mute
As any man, and love be far and high,
That else forsakes the topmost branch, a fruit
Found on the ground by every passer-by.

Not with libations, but with shouts and laughter
We drenched the altars of Love's sacred grove,
Shaking to earth green fruits, impatient after
The launching of the coloured moths of Love.
Love's proper myrtle and his mother's zone
We bound about our irreligious brows,
And fettered him with garlands of our own,
And spread a banquet in his frugal house.
Not yet the god has spoken; but I fear
Though we should break our bodies in his flame,
And pour our blood upon his altar, here
Henceforward is a grove without a name,
A pasture to the shaggy goats of Pan,[55]
Whence flee forever a woman and a man.

Only until this cigarette is ended,
A little moment at the end of all,
While on the floor the quiet ashes fall,
And in the firelight to a lance extended,
Bizarrely with the jazzing music blended,
The broken shadow dances on the wall,
I will permit my memory to recall
The vision of you, by all my dreams attended.
And then adieu,—farewell!—the dream is done.
Yours is a face of which I can forget
The colour and the features, every one,
The words not ever, and the smiles not yet;
But in your day this moment is the sun
Upon a hill, after the sun has set.

Once more into my arid days like dew,
Like wind from an oasis, or the sound
Of cold sweet water bubbling underground,
A treacherous messenger, the thought of you
Comes to destroy me; once more I renew
Firm faith in your abundance, whom I found
Long since to be but just one other mound
Of sand, whereon no green thing ever grew.
And once again, and wiser in no wise,
I chase your coloured phantom on the air,
And sob and curse and fall and weep and rise
And stumble pitifully on to where,
Miserable and lost, with stinging eyes,
Once more I clasp,—and there is nothing there.

No rose that in a garden ever grew,[56]
In Homer's[57] or in Omar's[58] or in mine,
Though buried under centuries of fine
Dead dust of roses, shut from sun and dew
Forever, and forever lost from view,
But must again in fragrance rich as wine
The grey aisles of the air incarnadine
When the old summers surge into a new.
Thus when I swear, "I love with all my heart,"
'Tis with the heart of Lilith[59] that I swear,
'Tis with the love of Lesbia[60] and Lucrece;[61]
And thus as well my love must lose some part
Of what it is, had Helen[62] been less fair,
Or perished young, or stayed at home in Greece.

When I too long have looked upon your face,[63]
Wherein for me a brightness unobscured
Save by the mists of brightness has its place,
And terrible beauty not to be endured,
I turn away reluctant from your light,
And stand irresolute, a mind undone,
A silly, dazzled thing deprived of sight
From having looked too long upon the sun.
Then is my daily life a narrow room
In which a little while, uncertainly,
Surrounded by impenetrable gloom,
Among familiar things grown strange to me
Making my way, I pause, and feel, and hark,
Till I become accustomed to the dark.

And you as well must die, belovèd dust,[64]
And all your beauty stand you in no stead;
This flawless, vital hand, this perfect head,
This body of flame and steel, before the gust
Of Death, or under his autumnal frost,
Shall be as any leaf, be no less dead
Than the first leaf that fell,—this wonder fled,
Altered, estranged, disintegrated, lost.
Nor shall my love avail you in your hour.
In spite of all my love, you will arise
Upon that day and wander down the air
Obscurely as the unattended flower,
It mattering not how beautiful you were,
Or how belovèd above all else that dies.

Let you not say of me when I am old,
In pretty worship of my withered hands
Forgetting who I am, and how the sands
Of such a life as mine run red and gold
Even to the ultimate sifting dust, "Behold,
Here walketh passionless age!"—for there expands
A curious superstition in these lands,
And by its leave some weightless tales are told.
In me no lenten wicks watch out the night;
I am the booth where Folly holds her fair;
Impious no less in ruin than in strength,
When I lie crumbled to the earth at length,
Let you not say, "Upon this reverend site
The righteous groaned and beat their breasts in prayer."

Oh, my belovèd, have you thought of this:[65]
How in the years to come unscrupulous Time,
More cruel than Death, will tear you from my kiss,
And make you old, and leave me in my prime?
How you and I, who scale together yet
A little while the sweet, immortal height
No pilgrim may remember or forget,
As sure as the world turns, some granite night
Shall lie awake and know the gracious flame
Gone out forever on the mutual stone;
And call to mind that on the day you came
I was a child, and you a hero grown?—
And the night pass, and the strange morning break
Upon our anguish for each other's sake!

As to some lovely temple, tenantless
Long since, that once was sweet with shivering brass,
Knowing well its altars ruined and the grass
Grown up between the stones, yet from excess
Of grief hard driven, or great loneliness,
The worshiper returns, and those who pass
Marvel him crying on a name that was,—
So is it now with me in my distress.
Your body was a temple to Delight;
Cold are its ashes whence the breath is fled;
Yet here one time your spirit was wont to move;
Here might I hope to find you day or night;
And here I come to look for you, my love,
Even now, foolishly, knowing you are dead.

Cherish you then the hope I shall forget
At length, my lord, Pieria?[66]—put away
For your so passing sake, this mouth of clay,
These mortal bones against my body set,
For all the puny fever and frail sweat
Of human love,—renounce for these, I say,
The Singing Mountain's memory, and betray
The silent lyre that hangs upon me yet?
Ah, but indeed, some day shall you awake,
Rather, from dreams of me, that at your side
So many nights, a lover and a bride,
But stern in my soul's chastity, have lain,
To walk the world forever for my sake,
And in each chamber find me gone again!

EXPLANATORY NOTES

Renascence and Other Poems

Renascence

1. Millay changed the spelling of the original title, "Renaissance," on the advice of Ferdinand Earle, editor of *The Lyric Year* anthology, where the poem was first published (see Introduction for details surrounding its publication and reception).
2. *I turned and looked another way:* Millay's original line, "I turned and looked the other way," appeared in *The Lyric Year* and *Renascence and Other Poems*; she revised it (and divided the poem into shorter stanzas) before publishing *Collected Lyrics* in 1939.
3. *The pitying rain began to fall:* Both the theme and some of the imagery in "Renascence" are reminiscent of Coleridge's *The Rime of the Ancient Mariner.* For example, as both the "Renascence" speaker and the mariner begin to ease out of their respective spiritual crises, they are refreshed by rain, then frightened by the subsequent storm. Consider these lines from Part V of Coleridge's poem: "And when I awoke, it rained. / . . . / I thought that I had died in sleep, / And was a blessed ghost. / . . . / And the coming wind did roar more loud / . . . / And the rain poured down from one black cloud; / The moon was at its edge . . ." and these (beginning with line 108) from Millay's poem: "The pitying rain began to fall; / . . . / For rain it hath a friendly sound / To one who's six feet under ground; / . . . / Upset each cloud's gigantic gourd / And let the heavy rain, down-poured / In one big torrent . . . / Before the wild wind's whistling lash / . . . / And the big rain in one black wave / Fell from the sky . . ."
4. *And scarce the friendly voice or face, / A grave is such a quiet place:* These lines echo one of Millay's favorite poems by Andrew Marvell, "To His Coy Mistress" (see *Letters*, #28): "The grave's a fine and quiet place, / but none, I think, do there embrace."

Interim

5. Millay added a stage direction—"A Man Speaks"—beneath the title of this poem before entering it in an intercollegiate poetry contest

that was judged by more established poets, including Robert Frost; it won first prize. It was later published in the *Vassar Miscellany* (July 1914) and in the *Forum*. Millay removed the stage direction before the poem appeared in *Renascence and Other Poems*.

The Suicide

6. Written in heroic couplets in the manner of Chaucer, Dryden, and Pope, this poem presents still another spiritual crisis, this time using the dialogue form (though not the pastoral theme) from Virgil's *Eclogues*.
7. *And "Father!" I cried, and clasped His knees, and wept:* An echo of the closing lines of George Herbert's "The Collar":

   But as I raved and grew more fierce and wild
   At every word,
   Methought I heard one calling, Child!
   And I replied, 'My Lord."

God's World

8. The intensity of this hymn to nature reflects Millay's closeness to the Romantic tradition; see Shelley's "Ode to a West Wind"—"O Wild West wind, thou breath of Autumn's being, / . . . / Oh, lift me as a wave, a leaf, a cloud!" (lines 53–54)—and the last stanza of Wordsworth's "Ode: Intimations of Immortality," which begins, "And O, ye Fountains, Meadows, Hills, and Groves, / Forbode not any severing of our loves!"

Ashes of Life

9. *And life goes on forever like the gnawing of a mouse,— / And tomorrow and tomorrow and tomorrow and tomorrow . . . :* A rather awkward allusion to Shakespeare's famous lines from *Macbeth*: "Tomorrow, and tomorrow, and tomorrow, / Creeps in this petty pace from day to day . . ." (5.5.19–20).

Witch-Wife

10. Here Millay offers her version of the alluring supernatural woman—found in myths, fairy tales, and ballads—who drives mortal men to distraction when they realize they cannot have her. This witch-wife is a more benign creature than many of her predecessors, including Keats's "La Belle Dame sans Merci."

When the Year Grows Old

11. Millay is recalling her beloved mother, Cora Millay.

Bluebeard

12. Millay bases her metaphor of dismissing a lover who invades her privacy on a fairy tale (see Introduction), a variation on the tale *Barbe-bleue* by Charles Perrault (1697), which is itself based on a true story, the crimes of the murderer Gilles de Retz.

A Few Figs from Thistles

First Fig

1. This is Millay's signature poem, probably the most quoted of all her works.

Recuerdo

2. Millay's title is Spanish for memory, "I remember," memento, or remembrance. In this poem, she recalls her experience with Salomón de la Selva, a Nicaraguan poet she met during her first summer in New York in 1913 when she was studying at Barnard and he was teaching modern Spanish poetry at Columbia University; their friendship lasted several years.

Macdougal Street

3. Millay knew this street well during her stay in New York; it was the location of the Provincetown Theatre where she first performed (in a play by Floyd Dell) in 1917.

The Singing-Woman from the Wood's Edge

4. This character is reminiscent of the heroine of a series of poems by Yeats: Crazy Jane, an irreverent but wise beggar who scorns conventional morality for a life based on instinct. See Introduction for a discussion of this poem.

Daphne

5. In Greek mythology, the daughter of a river god who escapes the amorous advances of Apollo by being changed into a laurel tree.
6. *Apollo:* Son of Zeus, Apollo was the Greek god of healing, archery, music, fine arts, and poetry who was notoriously unsuccessful in love.

To Kathleen

7. This poem was written for the youngest of the three Millay sisters, Kathleen, who aspired to be a writer and published both novels and poetry during her lifetime. She died in 1943, at age fifty-one. This poem was among a group of eight poems entitled "Personalities" that Millay sent to Allan Ross Macdougall in 1920. They were never published together, but two were included in *Letters*: a poem for Edith Wynne Matthison (#48n) and one for Macdougall (#70n). Four others appeared in separate Millay collections: "To Kathleen" and "To S. M." in *A Few Figs from Thistles*; a sonnet for Millay's sister Norma, "The light comes back with Columbine; she brings," in *The Harp-Weaver and Other Poems*; and part V of "From a Very Little Sphinx," written for Rollo Peters, in *Poems Selected for Young People*. The two remaining poems in the group, written for Ralph Roeder and Arthur Ficke, have never been published.

To S. M.

8. Written for Millay's friend Scudder Middleton (see previous note).
9. *Helen:* In Greek mythology, the daughter of Zeus and Leda whose abduction by Paris led to the Trojan War; throughout literature, she symbolizes female beauty and sexual attraction.
10. *Cleopatra:* An Egyptian queen (69–30 B.C.) known for her beauty and charm, colorfully portrayed in Shakespeare's *Antony and Cleopatra.*
11. *Sappho:* One of the most famous lyric poets (b. 612 B.C.), called the tenth muse by classical writers. The leader of a group of young women devoted to poetry and music on her native island of Lesbos, she was married and had a daughter. According to legend, she threw herself into the sea after the youth Phaon rejected her attentions. Millay mentions Sappho in several of her poems (including "Sappho Crosses the Dark River into Hades" in *Wine from These Grapes*). In a comment (published in *Poetry*'s August 1924 issue) that became known among Millay's critics as a premature and overzealous judgment, Harriet Monroe named Millay "the greatest woman poet since Sappho . . ." and predicted that the best of her lyrics would "probably be cherished as the richest, most precious gift of song which any woman since the immortal Lesbian has offered to the world." In fact, Millay owned a bronze bust of Sappho, which still stands on a marble pedestal in the living room at Steepletop as it did during the poet's lifetime.
12. *Cressid:* A character from medieval legend who vowed eternal fidelity

to Troilus but betrayed him for the Greek Diomedes; her name has become synonymous with infidelity.

13. *Dido:* In Virgil's *Aeneid*, the founder and queen of Carthage; she fell in love with Aeneas but killed herself when the gods ruled that he must leave Carthage to start his own nation in Italy.

The Philosopher

14. *And what am I, that I should love / So wisely and so well?:* A variation on Shakespeare's line at the end of *Othello*, when Othello says, ". . . then must you speak of one that loved not wisely but too well . . ."

Love, though for this you riddle me with darts

15. Millay employs a traditional approach here when she addresses Love, personified as a Cupid figure. The accusing voice in the poem is reminiscent of Donne's in the sonnet "Death Be Not Proud," though Millay changes her tone to provide an amusing twist in the final couplet.

Oh, think not I am faithful to a vow

16. While the paradox here, circling from the first line to Millay's final couplet—"So wanton, light and false, my love, are you, / I am most faithless when I most am true"—calls to mind Shakespeare's sonnet #138, "When my love swears she is made of truth, / I do believe her though I know she lies," it most certainly echoes Donne's concluding lines in "The Indifferent": ". . . Since you will be true, / You will be true to them who are false to you."

I shall forget you presently, my dear

17. *I will protest you with my favourite vow:* In this sonnet, one of Millay's most successful mergers of the traditional and the modern, her words echo Shakespeare's line from *Hamlet*: "The lady protests too much, methinks" (3.2.254).

Second April

1. Millay originally called this collection *Poems*, then *A Stalk of Fennel*, before changing it to *Second April* (see *Letters*, #67). The book's dedication, to her friend and benefactor, reads: "To my beloved friend Caroline B. Dow."

Spring

2. Millay's bitter tone here is a departure from most of her early poems, as is the free verse form. The poem—which suffers from both unfortunate word choices like "stickily" and flat, unoriginal pronouncements like "I know what I know" and "The smell of the earth is good"—resounds with echoes, first of Eliot (the opening to his once revolutionary *Waste Land* reads "April is the cruelest month, . . .") then of Shakespeare. Millay's concluding lines "April / Comes like an idiot, babbling and strewing flowers" recalls scenes from *Hamlet*: Ophelia's descent into madness—when she chattered on about flowers and herbs to Laertes (4.5.199–201, 204–210) and the Queen's subsequent description of her drowning surrounded by garlands of flowers (4.7.190–200). Other wording in Millay's poem—"But what does that signify? / . . . / Life in itself / Is nothing"—calls to mind Macbeth's unforgettable metaphor for life: "It is a tale / told by an idiot, full of sound and fury, / Signifying nothing" (*Macbeth*, 5.5.26–28).

The Blue-Flag in the Bog

3. A blue iris that grows in marshy areas.
4. Millay's voice and child's point of view here reflect Blake's *Songs of Innocence*; the dramatic situation resembles her earlier narrative, "The Suicide."
5. *All's well and all's well!:* The merger of nature (the blue-flag) and the spiritual realm (heaven)—a theme found in many poetic movements, including Romantic and Pre-Raphaelite—results in the speaker's optimism and sense of well-being at the end of the poem. The line itself echoes Robert Browning's line, from "Pippa Passes": "God's in his Heaven—All's right with the world!" as well as the title of a Shakespeare comedy, *All's Well That Ends Well* (c. 1602).

Journey

6. After this poem was published in the *Forum* in May 1913, Millay wrote to Arthur Ficke, "And you might tell me what you think of my 'Journey.' . . . It is neither sublime nor rotten, so there is a middle ground" (*Letters*, #25).

The Bean-Stalk

7. In 1920, Millay received a $100 prize from *Poetry* magazine for this poem, in which she addresses the giant from the well-known chil-

dren's tale "Jack and the Beanstalk," telling him that her trade is building "bean-stalks" (writing poems).

Passer Mortuus Est

8. Latin phrase that translates to "the sparrow is dead."
9. *Lesbia with her sparrow:* Lesbia, who appears in the love lyrics of the Roman poet Catullus (87–54 B.C.), is based on Clodia, a beautiful, talented young Roman woman (the sister of Cicero's archenemy, Clodius Pulcher) whose inconstant love inspired many of his works. Millay's first stanza alludes to Catullus's poem #3, in which he recounts the death of Lesbia's pet sparrow in a mock dirge (he uses poetic form and diction usually reserved for the death of a king or other high-level official to commemorate the death of the bird). At the end of Catullus's poem, he blames the sparrow for making his lover's eyes red from crying. Millay begins her poem with a dramatic opening line ("Death devours all lovely things"), then—still alluding to the death of the sparrow—acknowledges that time drains emotion from memory (stanza two). At last, perhaps echoing Clodia's attitude toward Catullus, Millay playfully jabs at her former lover by raising a philosophical dilemma: Does lost love qualify as love at all?

Song of a Second April

10. The quiet lyricism and note of longing here are reminiscent of A. E. Housman, who expressed admiration for Millay's work (see *Letters*, #110n).

The Poet and His Book

11. Here Millay treats a common literary theme: the artist's desire to be immortalized through her art. During Edmund Wilson's last visit to Steepletop in August 1948, Millay recited this poem with great emotion for him and his wife. Wilson describes the scene in "Epilogue, 1952" in his *Shores of Light* (New York: Vintage Books, 1961).
12. *Sexton:* A church worker who frequently serves as a gravedigger.

To a Poet that Died Young

13. This poem is addressed to Tennyson, who died in 1892 (the year of Millay's birth) at age eighty-three. Millay explains the title in her paradoxical line, "Growing old is dying young" (line 18). Even with all the evidence to the contrary, particularly Millay's references to Tennyson's poetry (noted below), it is possible to interpret this poem as if it were addressed to Wordsworth: for example, he was poet

laureate before Tennyson, shared a happier "fate" (line 3) because his reputation stayed intact and, finally, never lived to see Tennyson when, as the new laureate, he "sat and gossipped with [the] queen" (line 22). The mention of Shelley (line 27) also brings Wordsworth to mind.

14. *England's Laureate:* Tennyson was poet laureate from 1850 until his death; he was succeeded by Alfred Austin, who never achieved the fame Tennyson enjoyed.
15. *Thickly crusts the blackest moss:* An allusion to the first line of Tennyson's early poem "Mariana": "With blackest moss the flower plots / Were thickly crusted, one and all."
16. *Floats the boat that is forgot / None the less to Camelot:* Refers to the story of Lancelot and Elaine from Arthurian legend. In *Idylls of the King,* Tennyson recasts the story from Malory's *Morte d'Arthur* (c. 1469) in which Elaine tricks Lancelot into fathering a son by assuming the likeness of his beloved Queen Guinevere. Tennyson's Elaine is "the lily maid of Astolat" who dies of her overbearing love for the gallant knight. After her death, her body floats down the river in a barge, a lily in her right hand and a letter proclaiming Lancelot's innocence in the other. When the barge reaches Camelot, King Arthur orders that the letter be read aloud, then directs that she should be given a queen's burial. Tennyson modifies this story in "The Lady of Shalott," in which an unnamed "fairy" lady living on the island of Shalott, up the river from Camelot, knows she will be cursed to die if she leaves her tower and goes there. After seeing Lancelot pass by, she finds a boat, writes her name on the prow and follows him, singing her last song as she moves along. As she enters the domain of Camelot, she dies, then floats silently through the city. The people are afraid, but Lancelot recognizes her and calms them.
17. *Many a bard's untimely death / Lends unto his verses breath; / Here's a song was never sung: / Growing old is dying young:* Millay is suggesting that, ironically, the work of poets who die young may receive more attention than that of poets who live longer, in that older poets may find their reputation "dying young," before they do. She is alluding to Tennyson's greatly diminished reputation during the second half of his career.
18. *Thalia:* The Greek muse of comedy and pastoral poetry. Here, Millay is probably referring to another Thalia, one of the three goddesses called Charities (or Graces, in Roman mythology), who embodied beauty and charm; Thalia personified luxuriant beauty, which would be affected by the aging process Millay describes.

19. *Shelley's gold:* Shelley's talent, revealed in his poetry; Millay wonders if Shelley, who died at thirty, would have produced the same quality poetry had he lived to be old.

Elaine

20. See note #16 above.

Mariposa

21. Spanish for "butterfly." This poem is based on the carpe diem (seize the day) theme that originated in Latin poetry and was popularized in Robert Herrick's "To the Virgins, to Make Much of Time" and Andrew Marvell's "To His Coy Mistress." Here Millay entreats her lover to let her love him, thereby following the example of the butterfly who is enjoying a short life before death comes. The poem was originally included in her play, *The Lamp and the Bell* (1921), a costume drama based on a fairy tale written for a Vassar Alumnae Association event.

The Little Hill

22. Gethsemane is the garden or orchard near Jerusalem, at the foot of the Mount of Olives, the scene of Christ's agony.

Doubt No More that Oberon

23. *Oberon:* King of the fairies in medieval legend; he appears in mythology and literature (see, for example, Robert Herrick's rollicking poem "Oberon's Feast" and Shakespeare's *A Midsummer Night's Dream*).
24. *Pan:* In Greek mythology, the god of pastures, forests, flocks, and herds; he is a satyr (a man with goat's ears, horns, tail, and legs) who plays a flute he invented by joining seven reeds together.
25. *Death to fauns and death to fays:* Fauns are mythical creatures with tails, horns, goat's legs and hooves, and furry, pointed ears; fays are elves or fairies who are deities of fate.

Lament

26. Millay develops this theme—the mother who puts her own needs and feelings aside to sacrifice for her children—in her later, more effective fantasy poem, "The Ballad of the Harp-Weaver."

The Death of Autumn

27. The Romantic influence is evident here with a personified Beauty and strong echoes of Keats's "To Autumn": "Where are the songs

of spring? . . . / Think not of them, thou hast thy music too—" (lines 23–24).

ODE TO SILENCE

28. Here Millay constructs a rather uneven free ode in her search for Silence, whom she names the sister of the nine muses who has left them for an unknown destination. The poet, who longs for the presence of Silence, seeks her in Hell, in Heaven, then in Memory, where she finds only a trace (a "shadow," lines 132–33) that quickly fades. As she becomes frustrated in her search, she angrily reminds the "sister" muses that Silence existed before and after the sound of their songs and suggests that Silence may have died. At last, the poet appeals to the muse of harmony and lyric poetry, Euterpe (line 152, see note #43 below) who assures her that Silence does exist, in Oblivion, which for Euterpe is "the madness of an unaccustomed mood" (line 163).

    Millay wrote this ode in 1919 in response to the noise and commotion of New York living; she mentions it in a letter to Walter Adolphe Roberts, then editor of *Ainslee's* magazine (who lent her his supposedly quiet apartment for two weeks while he was away):

    > I've not finished the ode—though I've done a good bit on it . . . you bum, the people downstairs do play the piano!—It's as bad as 19th Street for a truly music-loving population.—"I shall hate sweet music my whole life long"! (*Letters*, #52)

    In 1920, she sent the finished poem to Arthur Ficke, who made suggestions for revision. Though she agreed with his advice, it was too late to make changes and the ode was published in its original form (see *Letters*, #74).
29. *Clio:* Muse of heroic poetry and history.
30. *Calliope:* Muse of epic poetry and chief of the muses.
31. *Apollo:* See note #5 (for "Daphne") from *A Few Figs from Thistles*. Attended by the muses, Apollo was also the celestial musician.
32. *Thalia:* See note #18 above.
33. *Melpomene:* Muse of tragedy.
34. *Terpsichore:* Muse of dancing and the dramatic chorus.
35. *Demeter's daughter:* In lines 48–63, Millay alludes to the Greek myth of Demeter, goddess of fruitfulness, harvests, corn, marriage, and social order (sometimes called "earth mother"). When her daughter, Persephone, picked a flower in her native Sicily, the earth opened

and Hades kidnapped her and carried her to the underworld. In roaming the world to find her, Demeter neglected the earth, causing blight, drought, and famine. Hades agreed to return Persephone to her mother, but only for nine months of each year; the remaining three months—when Persephone stayed with Hades (as queen of the underworld) and her mother mourned her absence—became the earth's winter season.

36. *Persephone:* See previous note. Persephone was also known as the goddess of the reviving crops. The "seed" (line 48) is from the flower she carried into Hell and tried to plant there. (Millay may also be referring to the pomegranate seed eaten by Persephone that magically bound her to return to Hades.) Millay imagines that Silence "will be . . . found" with Persephone each winter in her loneliness, when she lives within "the unequivocable battlements of Hell" (lines 61–62).
37. *Zeus:* The supreme god of the ancient Greeks, who fathered many offspring with goddesses and mortal women (Persephone was one of his daughters).
38. *the Hill:* Calvary, where Jesus was crucified. See Millay's poem "The Little Hill."
39. *Mnemosene:* The goddess of memory and mother, by Zeus, of the nine muses.
40. *caryatides:* Sculptured female figures used as columns.
41. *Psyche's lamp:* Psyche was the mortal wife of the god of love, Eros (Cupid), who warned her not to gaze upon him. Curious to see him, she held a lamp over his sleeping form; a drop of oil fell on his shoulder and he awoke and flew away. In her search for him, Psyche died; Eros revived her and Zeus made her immortal.
42. *Pieria:* A Macedonian coast district at the base of Mt. Olympus known as the birthplace of Orpheus and the muses.
43. *Euterpe:* Muse of harmony and lyric poetry and patroness of joy and pleasure.
44. *Herakles* (Greek for Hercules): A mythical hero, son of Zeus, who performed many phenomenal tasks with his superhuman strength. Millay mentions his having "walked" in Hell because one of his tasks, or Labors, was to descend into Hades and seize the three-headed guard dog Cerberus.
45. *And he that loved Euridice too well:* Millay is referring to Orpheus, the musician son of Calliope (see note #30 above), whose wife, Euridice, was killed by a snake and sent to Hades. Distraught, Orpheus went into Hell to find her, charmed Hades with his music, and led her

back to earth. (When he disobeyed Hades's orders not to look back at her, however, she was returned to Hades forever.)

Memorial to D. C.

46. Dorothy Coleman, Millay's friend from Vassar, died suddenly in 1918.
47. *Persephone:* See notes #35 and #36 above.

Wild Swans

48. Millay's use of wild swans to represent the constant and ethereal beauty of nature in contrast to human inconsistencies follows Yeats's more developed poetic commentary in "The Wild Swans at Coole."

We talk of taxes, and I call you friend

49. *Isolde:* The heroine in the medieval story of *Tristan and Iseult*; her name appears is various forms, and the story itself varies. In every version, Isolde and Tristan drink a magic potion that causes them to love one another forever. (Millay refers to this character, spelled Isolt, and to Cressid and Elaine again in a later sonnet in which she criticizes her lover for reading about mythical women rather than acknowledging her sexual needs. (See "Since I cannot persuade you from this mood," *Fatal Interview*, sonnet VI.)
50. *Guinevere:* In Arthurian legend, King Arthur's wife and Lancelot's lover, who gave Arthur the illustrious Round Table as a wedding gift.
51. *the Table's ruin:* Here Millay makes reference to Guinevere's affair with Lancelot as the "ruin" of the Round Table. The story goes that Guinevere persuaded Lancelot to kill one of the Table's knights who had informed Arthur of her unfaithfulness.
52. *Francesca:* Millay alludes to a famous scene in the *Inferno* during Dante's visit to the second circle of carnal sinners, where Francesca da Rimini relates her story; married to an unattractive man, she fell in love with her husband's brother, Paolo, while they were reading the story of Lancelot together. This sonnet was published in the issue of the *Dial* (28 December 1918) under the title "Quanti Dolci Pensier, Quanti Disio," a reference to Dante's remark about Francesca as she begins to describe her love affair with Paolo: "What sweet thoughts, what desire brought these lovers to this unhappy end" (5: line 113).
53. *with the loud surf at her ear:* Francesca was from Rimini, a town on the northeast coast of Italy where she and Paolo fell in love.

Into the golden vessel of great song

54. In a letter written to Arthur Ficke in 1921, Millay wrote:

> The sonnet you asked me about—the one "There is no shelter in you anywhere" was written about you & about myself—we were both like that—but are not anymore. The "golden vessel of great song," also was written to you. My time, in those awful days after you went away to France, was a mist of thinking about you & writing sonnets to you.— . . . That day before you sailed,— I shall never forget it. You were the first man I ever kissed without first thinking that I should be sorry about it afterwards. . . . (*Letters*, #90)

Not with libations, but with shouts and laughter

55. *Pan:* See note #24 above.

No rose that in a garden ever grew

56. Millay further develops this sonnet's theme in "Women have loved before as I love now," a sonnet in which she allies herself with women from "lively chronicles of the past" who lived in the "day / When treacherous queens, with death upon the tread, / Heedless and wilful, took their knights to bed" (*Fatal Interview*, sonnet XXVI, lines 2, 12–14).
57. *Homer:* Ionian poet, generally accepted as the author of the *Iliad* and the *Odyssey*.
58. *Omar:* Omar Khayyam (d. 1123), the Persian astronomer-poet who wrote the celebrated series of quatrains, *The Rubaiyat of Omar Khayyam*.
59. *Lilith:* In the Old Testament, a spirit of the air who assumed the form of a beautiful woman to beguile and destroy. In Talmudic lore, she was Adam's wife before Eve.
60. *Lesbia:* See note #9 above.
61. *Lucrece:* In Roman legend, the devoted wife of Tarquinius Collatinus who was violated by the king's son and killed herself after declaring her dishonor to her father, her husband, and their friends.
62. *Helen:* See note #9 from *A Few Figs from Thistles*.

When I too long have looked upon your face

63. Comparing the light in her lover's face to the "brightness" of the sun, Millay reworks a common Petrarchan conceit that compares a

lover's eyes with the glare of sunlight. (Shakespeare reverses the conceit in "My mistress' eyes are nothing like the sun" [sonnet #130].) This sonnet was written for Arthur Ficke.

And you as well must die, belovèd dust

64. The saga that accompanies this sonnet all but overshadows its familiar theme—death's equalizing effect on human beings. In 1937, Millay wrote to Arthur Ficke:

> Arthur darling:
>
> This will be one of the most unpleasant letters you ever received, and I'm sorry. But it's time I got this matter off my chest and onto yours, where it belongs,—for it's all your fault, my dear, for asking such shockingly indiscreet questions. The sonnet was not written to you.
>
> When you came at me like a prosecuting attorney the other night in the LaBranches' gun-room, asking me so casually—and I at least six cocktails off my guard,—"To whom did you write that sonnet, Vince?" I glibly and immediately countered with the only name which in the circumstances it would not be indiscreet to mention: your own. To keep my loosened tongue from folly . . .
>
> Knowing as you so well know, my dear friend, how reticent, both by nature and by taste, concerning my own private affairs and the affairs of other people, I am, it is wrong of you to do these things to me. . . . If you love me as you say you do, it is very foolish. For don't you see, Artie darling, that in the circumstances it is impossible for me to be at ease with you, and that eventually just out of self-protection I shall avoid being with you wherever possible?
>
> I know that I must have hurt you. I'm so sorry. But it was no good letting it go like that. Because it couldn't stop there. Our two distinct and incompatible memories of that moment in the gun-room, would have twisted out of shape every word we ever said to each other again. (*Letters*, #210)

The letter is signed, "With love, Vincent." Eight years later, in the fall of 1945, when Ficke was gravely ill, Millay wrote him a letter that addressed the subject again, for the last time:

> Dear Arthur:
>
> I *did* write that sonnet to you, the one you asked me about.—I denied it at the time,—but what a hell of a time, and what a

> hell of a place to ask me about it! . . . Of course, you spoke in a voice so low that no one else could possibly have overheard you. But anyway. And besides, you sprang the question on me so suddenly . . . that it almost caught me off guard; it makes me furious. (A devil's-trick that is of yours too, Angel-in-all-else.)
>
> Perhaps, also, I didn't want you to know, for sure, how terribly, how sickeningly, in love with you I had been.
>
> And perhaps, also, I was still in love with you, or I shouldn't have cared.
>
> Well, anyway. The sonnet was the one beginning: "And you as well must die, beloved dust." In case you've forgotten. Which you haven't. (*Letters*, #241)

The letter was signed "Vincie." Ficke died on November 30 and Millay read the sonnet at his burial along with passages from Milton's "Lycidas," one of Ficke's favorite poems.

OH, MY BELOVÈD, HAVE YOU THOUGHT OF THIS

65. In this sonnet, written for Ficke, Millay modifies the carpe diem theme to provide a response of sorts to Shakespeare's "That time of year thou mayst in me behold" (sonnet #73).

CHERISH YOU THEN THE HOPE I SHALL FORGET

66. *Pieria:* See note #42 above. This theme—Millay's refusal to renounce her art for love—recurs throughout her poetry and prose.

INDEX OF TITLES AND FIRST LINES